Jeanne Jones'
Party Planner & Entertaining Diary

Illustrations and Design by
Michael Boedeker

101 Productions
San Francisco

Published by 101 Productions, Inc.
834 Mission Street
San Francisco, California 94103
Distributed to the book trade
in the United States by
Charles Scribner's Sons, New York.

ISBN 0-89286-156-8

*E*ntertaining is my favorite hobby as well as the basis of my career as a cookbook author and food consultant. For many years I have wanted to write a book on party planning in order to share with others my entertaining diary that makes party planning so much easier and so much more fun. Most of us at some time have had that panicky feeling a few days before a party of not remembering what we served for dinner the last time we entertained the same people — or not remembering the decor or even what we wore. Serving exactly the same menu with the same flowers on the table while wearing the same attire might be a bit embarrassing for both you and your guests. Keeping complete records of your parties eliminates these frustrating experiences.

When I told my accountant about my diary, he was equally excited because it is a wonderful way for clients to keep accurate records of their business entertaining, including the purpose of the party, the guests and the breakdown of the costs.

As everyone who has read my other books knows, I love to cook as well as to entertain. In this book I am also giving several menu suggestions, using recipes from my other books, for healthful and low-calorie as well as imaginative and delicious meals. You may be surprised to find that most of your friends will enjoy coming to your home even more when they do not feel they must give up eating either two days before or two days after one of your parties.

When planning a party, the first and most important thing to consider is the guest list. The type of party you give may differ greatly depending upon the guests you invite. For example, you may have an elderly friend who is a delightful conversationalist and would enjoy a small sit-down dinner but not a stand-up cocktail party.

When selecting guests for a small dinner party, I find it is sometimes more fun to combine people who do not see each other regularly and who are involved in totally different fields. Unless you are giving a very large party, it is often better not to send invitations, but instead to invite your guests by telephone and send a reminder a few days before the party, again giving them the date, time and place. This way, you get an immediate "yes" or "no" on your guest list and it is easier to assemble a compatible group. Also at this time you can find out about any special dietary needs of your guests, ranging from simple likes and dislikes to food allergies. (Remember, as a host or hostess you are attempting to entertain your guests rather than to reeducate them — or worse yet — make them sick!) If you are sending invitations, unless it is for an extremely large party, it is risky to put "regrets only." Often people are out of town and do not receive the invitations, therefore cannot regret and yet are still expected. When receiving an invitation yourself, it is important to always respond as quickly as possible, giving the host or hostess an opportunity to ask someone else in your place.

After determining the type of party you are going to give and inviting your guests, the next important consideration is the menu. Like the guest list, the menu is in part dictated by the type of party you are giving, as well as the amount of help you are going to have. If you are giving a dinner party by yourself without any additional help, it is extremely important to plan a menu that you can prepare ahead of time so that you are free to be with your guests. As the host or hostess you are not simply preparing a meal, you are entertaining your guests. Planning a menu that you can serve easily keeps you from making your guests nervous by continually jumping up from the table.

I prefer a sit-down dinner party for ten people over all other types of entertaining. It is a number large enough to create a real party atmosphere and yet small enough to allow your guests either to get better acquainted or to enjoy talking with old friends. Also, if you are entertaining an even number of men and women, it is easy to seat people at a table for ten, alternating the sexes. When I am giving this type of party without help I arrange the courses in such a way that I will be away from my guests as little as possible.

Sometimes I serve the first course in the living room with cocktails. When doing this, I serve an hors d'oeuvre or appetizer such as small seafood crêpes, a small quiche, or oysters on the half shell. Serving soup in a mug to your guests before seating them at table is an unusual approach to the first course; this also permits you to graciously remove cocktail glasses and hors d'oeuvre so that you will not have to clear the area after dinner

if you are planning to return for coffee and after-dinner drinks.

Another approach is to seat your guests to their first course, which may be an appetizer, soup or salad, and then ask them to help themselves to their entree course. This gives you an opportunity to clear the table of the first course and tidy up the kitchen while your guests are serving themselves the entree. Then as you later remove their dinner plates, it is very easy to rinse each plate and put it in the dishwasher as it is being cleared from the table; you have thus eliminated a horrendous mess in the kitchen when the party is over. For a party of this type, I always serve a dessert at the table, such as poached fruit, fresh fruit and cheese, or a cold soufflé. By serving dinner in this manner, you are not away from your guests very much and yet the mood is more formal than at an entire meal served buffet style. Also when I am entertaining alone, I always ask one of my guests to serve the wine for me.

When giving a more formal dinner party with additional help, let your imagination run wild while planning the menu. Always include at least one dish you have never served before. Offering something brand new at a dinner party is far more exciting than sticking with the old favorites, just as it is more fun to wear something new.

I always love to have one course that is unusual and served in dishes not often used, such as artichoke bowls filled with a chilled soup on artichoke plates. After serving artichokes or any "messy" course, finger bowls for your guests are important, and certainly add a lovely touch to a formal dinner party.

Whenever using finger bowls, change your guests' napkins afterwards. What could be more uncomfortable than a soggy napkin in someone's lap for the duration of the meal.

Giving a party of any size can be lots of fun rather than just lots of work if you plan ahead properly. It is impossible to plan a menu, to shop, to cook and to give a party all on the same day. That is, it is impossible if you want to enjoy the party yourself. Entertaining should be exciting rather than exhausting. A good rule of thumb in party planning, whether for a formal dinner party or a casual backyard barbecue, is to plan your menu two to four days before the party and if possible do most of your shopping on the same day, except for last minute purchases such as fresh seafood and certain vegetables. Then, the day before the party prepare as many dishes as possible, leaving only those that require last-minute preparation until just before the party begins.

After planning your menu, it is equally important to decide how you will serve it. First check the table linens you plan to use, the condition of the tablecloth, napkins, etc. If you are giving a more casual party with paper cloths and napkins, they should be on the shopping list of things to purchase well in advance. Next consider your china, silver and serving pieces. If you do not have enough china in the same pattern for all your guests, mix patterns. It is less expensive than renting, less trouble than borrowing, and often creates a more interesting table. The amount of stemware on the table depends on the number of wines served. If possible include a water goblet as well as wine glasses so that any guest not wishing to drink wine with the meal does not have to ask for water. Having the appropriate serving pieces for everything you plan to serve is not necessary. It is sometimes fun to use innovative containers such as large bowls filled with crushed ice for wine coolers and chilled soup tureens for salad. I have even filled large wine goblets with salad for luncheons. Always chill the salad plates or bowls in the freezer so that they are very cold when the salad is served. On occasion I also chill the salad forks.

Flowers and table decorations should be a reflection of your own style and appropriate for the type of party you are having. There are no longer unbreakable rules for table settings; always remember, however, to keep flowers or other decorative centerpieces low enough so that guests can see each other easily across the table.

Lighting is also important. Extremely bright lights for dining are unkind to both guests and food. While candlelight is flattering to both, make certain it provides light adequate to see both the food and each other.

Place cards are important if your party is for more than four persons. Nothing creates more confusion than everyone standing around the table wondering where to sit. If you are having a very large party, you should consider a seating chart so that your guests do not have to wander around looking for their place cards.

Party favors are fun and can be as elegant or whimsical as you wish. For ladies' luncheons I often tie the place cards to bud vases filled with flowers and give them to my guests as they leave. Hand-lettered menus add a personal touch to the table decor and also make nice favors.

Keeping records of your parties not only provides you with a marvelous diary of all of your past entertaining; such a book is also useful in planning future parties. The diary pages in this book include spaces for listing all of the information you might wish to record. There are even seating charts so that you can avoid seating a guest by the same person each time you entertain. A breakdown of both budgeted and actual costs will be helpful in estimating expenses for future parties. The records you keep can be as simple or as elaborate as you wish. By keeping records you will not only avoid the repetitions I mentioned earlier, such as serving the same food or wearing the same clothes; you will add variety to your parties in many ways such as using different linens, china, centerpieces, or perhaps even serving in a different area of the house. You quickly will find that keeping this entertaining diary will motivate you to do still more entertaining—and that you will enjoy planning your own parties more than you ever have.

Jeanne Jones

Brunch Menu (For Four)

Ramos Fizz (with gin)
Ramos Fizzle (without gin)
Green Eggs and Ham en Croustade
Fresh Fruit
Broiled Bananas
Coffee

This brunch menu is applicable to almost any kind of party. It can be used for an elegant brunch in a very formal setting or for a child's birthday party with a copy of Dr. Suess' book, Green Eggs and Ham, the table center-piece. I have even adapted this menu for a Sunday night supper, substituting champagne or sparkling cider for the Ramos Fizz.

RAMOS FIZZ (with gin)
RAMOS FIZZLE (without gin)

2 cups non-fat milk
2 tablespoons liquid
   fructose
2 tablespoons fresh lemon
   juice
1 teaspoon orange flower
   water
2 egg whites
1/2 cup soda water
3 ounces gin (optional)

1. Put all ingredients in a
blender container and
blend until smooth and
frothy.
2. Pour over ice in four tall
chilled glasses. Additional
soda water may be added if
desired.
Makes 4 servings.

GREEN EGGS AND HAM EN CROUSTADE

1 loaf whole-wheat bread,
   unsliced
2 tablespoons butter or
   corn-oil margarine,
   melted
8 eggs
1/2 cup low-fat milk
1/2 cup chopped fresh
   parsley
1/4 cup chopped fresh
   chives or green onion
   tops
1/2 teaspoon dried
   tarragon
1/2 teaspoon salt
1/8 teaspoon white pepper
1 tablespoon butter or
   corn-oil margarine
1 cup chopped cooked ham
1 tablespoon finely chopped
   fresh chives or green
   onion tops for garnish
6 parsley sprigs for garnish

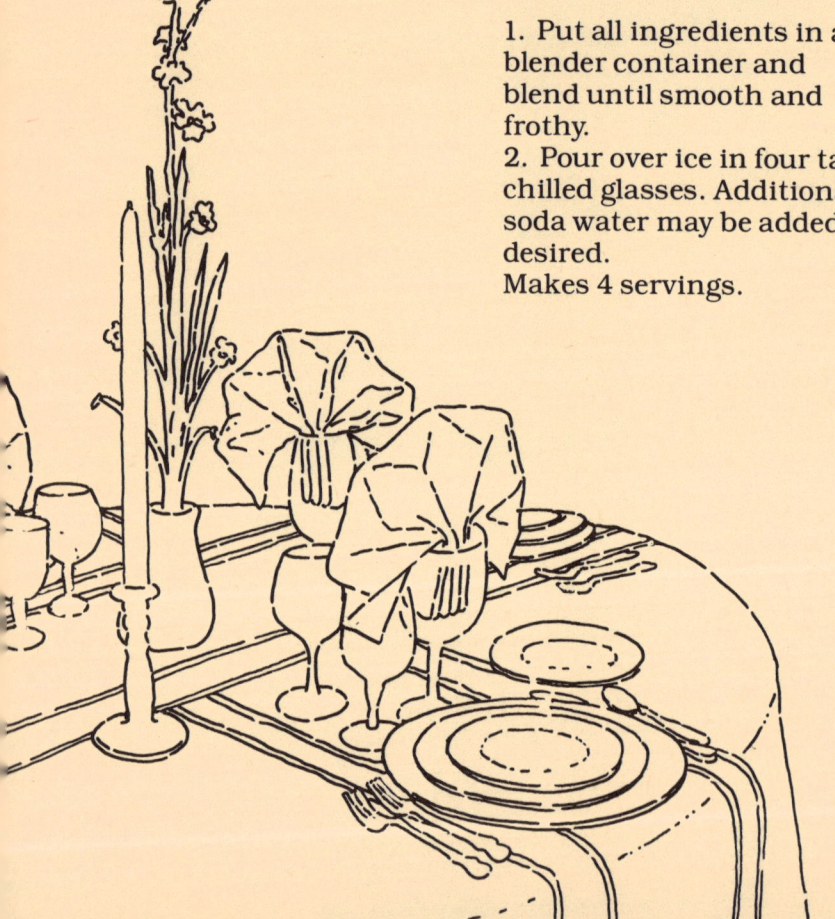

1. Preheat the oven to 325°.
2. Slice the top crust off of the loaf of bread. Carefully hollow out the loaf leaving walls 3/4 inch thick (I keep the bread crumbs in a sealed bag in the freezer to use in other recipes calling for whole-wheat bread crumbs).
3. Using a pastry brush, evenly apply the melted butter or margarine to the entire croustade. Place it on a cookie sheet in the preheated 325° oven for about 25 minutes or until it is well toasted. Remove to a serving platter and keep warm.
4. Put the eggs in a bowl and beat them until they are frothy.

5. Put the milk, parsley, chives, tarragon, salt and white pepper into a blender container and blend until smooth in texture. Put the green mixture into the eggs and mix thoroughly.
6. Melt the butter or margarine in a large skillet and heat the skillet well before adding the eggs.
7. Add the egg mixture and reduce the heat, stirring the eggs constantly until they are almost set. Add the ham and cook until eggs are the desired consistency. Be careful not to overcook the eggs as it makes them too dry.
8. Remove the eggs from the heat and spoon them into the croustade which has been placed on a serving platter.
9. Sprinkle the chopped chives over the top of the eggs and decorate the platter with sprigs of parsley.
Makes 4 servings.

BROILED BANANAS

2 large, not too ripe, bananas
1 tablespoon butter or corn-oil margarine, melted
Ground cinnamon

1. Peel the bananas and slice in half lengthwise.
2. Put the banana halves, cut side up, in a large baking dish or on a cookie sheet.
3. Brush the melted butter or margarine over them using a pastry brush.
4. Place the bananas under the broiler until lightly browned.
5. Lightly sprinkle the tops of the bananas with ground cinnamon.
Makes 4 servings.

*L*uncheon Menu (For Six)

Mock Boula Boula
Curried Chicken Salad in Lettuce Bowls
Cinnamon Popovers
Cold Orange Soufflé
Coffee or Tea

This luncheon menu is unique in that most of the items can be prepared the day before. Then, while you are putting the finishing touches on your salad, you can be reheating the Mock Boula Boula and heating the popovers. Your gorgeous soufflé will be in the refrigerator all ready for you to bring it in dramatically for dessert.

MOCK BOULA BOULA

2 cups beef stock
3 cups green peas, fresh or
    fresh frozen
1/4 teaspoon white pepper
1/8 teaspoon salt
1 teaspoon fructose
1 tablespoon corn-oil
    margarine
1 cup non-fat milk
1/2 cup sherry

1. In a saucepan combine
the beef stock, peas, white
pepper, salt and fructose
and bring to a boil.
2. Reduce heat, cover and
simmer 3–5 minutes or
until the peas are tender.
3. Pour the peas and all the
liquid in the pan into a
blender container.
4. Add all other ingredients
and blend until smooth in
texture.

*This soup is good hot or
cold. If you wish to reheat
it, do not allow it to come to
a boil. Boula Boula is a
classic soup combining
fresh peas and turtle. Because this recipe omits the
turtle, I call it "Mock"
Boula Boula.*
Makes 6 servings.

CURRIED CHICKEN SALAD IN LETTUCE BOWLS

6 small heads Bibb (Boston or butter) lettuce
3/4 cup chopped walnuts
4 tablespoons shredded coconut
2 cups (1 16-ounce can) drained pineapple chunks packed in natural juice
4 cups diced cold cooked chicken
1 cup Curry Dressing, recipe follows

1. Wash the lettuce and remove the hearts, being careful not to tear the outer leaves (the lettuce "bowls"). Tear three or four of the hearts into bite-sized pieces (approximately 5 cups of torn lettuce). Dry thoroughly and chill. Do this as much in advance as possible so that the lettuce "bowls" and torn lettuce are dry, cold and crisp.
2. Preheat the oven to 350°. Spread the walnuts evenly on a cookie sheet and place in the oven for 10–12 minutes or until well toasted, *watching them carefully because they burn easily.* Set aside. Then place the shredded coconut in a pie pan in the oven for 5–10 minutes or until a light golden brown. Watch carefully because it will burn easily. Set aside.
3. Combine the torn lettuce, toasted walnuts, pineapple chunks, chicken and Curry Dressing and mix thoroughly.
4. Divide the salad evenly into the 6 lettuce "bowls," placing each lettuce "bowl" on a chilled dinner-size plate.
5. Sprinkle the toasted coconut evenly over the tops of the salads.
Makes 6 servings.

CURRY DRESSING

3/4 cup sour cream
4 tablespoons mayonnaise
1/2 teaspoon curry powder
1/8 teaspoon powdered ginger
1/2 teaspoon salt

1. Put all ingredients in a blender container and blend until smooth.
Makes 1 cup.

CINNAMON POPOVERS

4 egg whites, at room temperature
1 cup low-fat milk, at room temperature
1 cup all-purpose flour
1/4 teaspoon fructose
1/2 teaspoon ground cinnamon
2 tablespoons unsalted butter or corn-oil margarine, melted

1. Preheat the oven to 450°.
2. Put all ingredients in a blender container and blend at medium speed for 15 seconds. *Do not overmix.*
3. Pour the batter into 6 3-1/2-inch custard cups that have been well sprayed with a non-stick coating. (Only non-stick spray will prevent the popovers from sticking; butter or margarine won't do the job.)
4. Bake in the 450° oven for 20 minutes. Reduce the heat to 350° and bake 20 more minutes. Serve immediately, or you may cool to room temperature, wrap in foil and freeze. Then reheat at 350° for 12–15 minutes before serving.
Makes 6 popovers.

COLD ORANGE SOUFFLÉ

2 envelopes (2 scant tablespoons) unflavored gelatin
1 cup cold water
2 egg yolks, at room
  temperature
2 6-ounce cans frozen un-
  sweetened orange juice
  concentrate, thawed
1 teaspoon vanilla extract
8 egg whites, at room
  temperature
1/2 cup fructose
1 cup skimmed evaporated
  milk, chilled
1 tablespoon freshly grated
  orange peel for garnish

1. Fold a sheet of waxed paper in half lengthwise and wrap around the top of a 6-inch (1 quart) soufflé dish to form a waxed-paper collar that extends at least 4 inches above the rim of the dish. Secure the collar with tape.

2. Soften the gelatin in the cold water and allow to stand for 5 minutes.

3. Beat the egg yolks with a mixer or wire whisk until they are thick and foamy. Beat in the softened gelatin.

4. Pour the mixture into the top of a double boiler and place over simmering water. Cook, stirring constantly, until the gelatin has completely dissolved. *Do not allow the mixture to come to a boil.*

5. Remove the pan from the heat and stir in the thawed orange juice concentrate and vanilla extract.

6. Pour the mixture into a large mixing bowl and refrigerate until thickened to a syrupy consistency, about 20 minutes.

7. Beat the egg whites until they are frothy. Slowly add 1/2 cup of fructose and continue beating until the egg whites are stiff but not dry; set aside.

8. In another bowl, beat the chilled milk until it has doubled in volume.

9. Fold the whipped milk mixture gently but thoroughly into the orange juice mixture, using a rubber spatula. Fold in the beaten egg whites, folding until no streaks of white show.

10. Pour the soufflé mixture into the collared soufflé dish and refrigerate for at least 4 hours before removing the collar and serving the soufflé.

11. Lightly sprinkle the top with grated orange peel for garnish.

Makes 16 servings.

The drama of this soufflé is its size. After a luncheon for six, you will have left-overs to serve your family dessert that evening. Or refrigerate and serve the following day.

Fiesta Dinner (For Eight)

**Fake Guacamole Dip
with Toasted Tortilla Triangles
Gazpacho
Chicken Enchiladas
Mexican Rice Pilaf
South-of-the-Border Fruit Kebabs
Mexican Coffee**

*This Fiesta Dinner can be
served very informally if
you are doing it by your-
self. It can also be turned
into a served sit-down
dinner if desired.*

When entertaining without additional help, offer your guests the Fake Guacamole Dip with Toasted Tortilla Triangles with their cocktails before dinner. Then before seating your guests at table, bring in the Gazpacho in chilled mugs. While your guests are drinking their soup, you can clear the cocktail glasses and hors d'oeuvre from the area. The Chicken Enchiladas and Mexican Rice Pilaf can be placed in serving dishes on a buffet table so that your guests may help themselves before sitting down at the table.

When your guests have finished the entree, remove the dinner plates, replacing them with dessert plates. Then bring the South-of-the-Border Fruit Kebabs to the table, letting each guest help himself to dessert.

When doing a Fiesta Dinner, I like to have my guests come back to the living room for Mexican Coffee. I make Mexican Coffee by adding small amount of cinnamon to regular coffee!

FAKE GUACAMOLE DIP

1 pound fresh asparagus
1 tablespoon fresh lemon
   juice
1-1/2 tablespoons finely
   chopped onion
1 medium tomato, chopped
1 teaspoon salt
1/4 teaspoon ground
   cumin
1/4 teaspoon chili powder
1/8 teaspoon garlic powder
Dash Tabasco sauce
1/2 cup sour cream
1 envelope (1 scant tablespoon) unflavored gelatin
1/4 cup water

1. Wash the asparagus and
break off the tough ends.
Cut the spears into 1-inch
pieces and cook in a
steamer until just fork
tender, about 4 minutes.
2. Cool the cooked as-
paragus to room tempera-
ture. Put the cooled as-
paragus and all other
ingredients, except the
gelatin and water, into a
blender container and
blend until smooth.
3. Put the gelatin in a small
saucepan and add the
water. Allow to soften for 5
minutes.

4. Place the pan on low
heat, stirring constantly,
until the gelatin is com-
pletely dissolved. *Do not
allow to come to a boil.*
5. Add the dissolved gelatin
to the blender container
and blend on low speed
until thoroughly mixed.
6. Pour the "guacamole" in
a bowl and refrigerate until
firm.
Makes 2 cups.

TOASTED TORTILLA
TRIANGLES

12 corn tortillas
Salt

1. Preheat the oven to 400°.
2. Cut each tortilla into 6
pie-shaped pieces.
3. Spread half of the tortilla
triangles on a cookie sheet
and salt lightly.
4. Bake them in the pre-
heated 400° oven for 10
minutes.
5. Remove from the oven,
turn each one over and return them to the oven for 3
more minutes. Remove
from the sheet and set
aside.
6. Place the remaining tortilla triangles on the cookie
sheet and repeat the
process.
Makes 72 triangles.

CHICKEN ENCHILADAS

1 tablespoon corn oil
1 large onion, chopped
1-1/2 teaspoons salt
1 tablespoon chili powder
1/2 teaspoon ground
   cumin
3 medium tomatoes, peeled
   and diced
2 cups chopped cooked
   chicken
1/2 cup chicken stock
1-1/2 cups grated sharp
   Cheddar cheese
8 corn tortillas, warmed

1. Preheat the oven to 350°.
2. Heat the oil in a skillet.
Add the chopped onion and
cook until tender.
3. Add the salt, chili powder and cumin and mix
well.
4. Add the tomatoes,
chicken and chicken stock,
mix well and cook for 5
minutes on low heat.
5. Add 3/4 cup of the
grated cheese to the mix-
ture and mix thoroughly.
Spoon the enchilada mix-
ture evenly down the center
of each tortilla.

6. Roll the warm tortilla around the warm cheese mixture and place, seam side down, in a greased 7- by 12-inch baking dish. Spoon any remaining sauce over the enchiladas in the dish evenly and sprinkle the remaining 3/4 cup of grated cheese over the tops of the 8 enchiladas.

7. Cover the baking dish and bake in the preheated 350° oven for 30 minutes. Makes 8 servings.

MEXICAN PILAF

3 tablespoons corn oil
2 garlic buds, minced
1 cup long-grain white rice
1 medium onion, thinly
    sliced
2 cups chicken stock,
    boiling
1 teaspoon dried oregano,
    crushed
1/2 teaspoon chili powder
1/2 teaspoon ground
    cumin
1/4 teaspoon freshly
    ground black pepper
1/4 teaspoon salt

1. Preheat the oven to 400°.
2. Heat the corn oil in a cured heavy iron skillet.
3. Add the garlic, rice and onion and cook, stirring frequently, until browned.
4. Combine the hot chicken stock with all remaining ingredients and mix well.
5. Put the rice mixture in a casserole dish with a tight-fitting lid.
6. Add the stock mixture and mix well.
7. Cover and place in the preheated 400° oven for 40 minutes.
8. Remove from the oven and allow to stand, covered, for 10 minutes before serving.
Makes 8 servings.

SOUTH-OF-THE-BORDER FRUIT KEBABS

2 cups cubed fresh pine-
    apple, or 1 16-ounce can
    of pineapple chunks
    packed in natural juice,
    drained
2 bananas, sliced in 1/2-
    inch pieces
2 large papayas, peeled and
    sliced in 1-inch pieces
2 large mangoes, peeled
    and cubed, or 2 large
    oranges, peeled and
    cubed
16 wooden skewers

1. Place the variety of fruits alternately on the skewers.
2. Serve each guest two kebabs for dessert.
Makes 8 servings.

MEXICAN COFFEE

Add a small amount of ground cinnamon to regular coffee.

Formal Dinner Party (For Ten)

Artichoke Bowls with Cold Consommé
Coq au Vin with Brown Sauce
Mystery Pilaf
Tarragon Baked Tomatoes
Crêpes Suzette
Coffee or Tea

Pouilly Fuissé
Champagne

This menu can be prepared easily without additional help. To serve it formally, however, it is necessary to have at least one person serving the table.

When giving a formal dinner party, the first course should not be placed on the table until after the guests are seated. I like to use service plates with the napkin folded on top of the plate, then place the first course on the service plate. When removing

the first course from the table, the service plate should be removed and replaced with the plate containing the entree. After serving artichoke bowls, I like to remove them and follow with finger bowls. After the guests have used the finger bowls, the napkins should also be changed, so that everyone does not have to keep damp napkins in his lap for the rest of the meal.

I prefer to serve the entree on the plates rather than passing each dish for the guests to serve themselves; however this is just a personal preference. When the entree is removed from the table, all other items on the table such as individual salt and pepper shakers and bread plates should also be removed before serving dessert.

It is fun to do Crêpes Suzette either on the table or on a side table so that your guests can watch the preparation. I like to serve a chilled dry white wine with this menu, and champagne with the Crêpes Suzette.

ARTICHOKE BOWLS WITH COLD CONSOMMÉ

10 artichokes
2 garlic buds, peeled and halved
1 thick lemon slice
1/2 teaspoon salt
French Dressing, recipe follows
1 quart Consommé Madrilene, recipe follows
3/4 cup sour cream
5 teaspoons caviar
1-1/2 cups additional sour cream

1. Wash the artichokes well and pull off tough outer leaves. Holding each artichoke by its stem, cut the tips off the leaves with scissors. When trimming the tops, start at the bottom of the artichoke and work your way to the top in a spiral pattern. Trim off the stem, turn the artichoke upside down and press firmly to open it up as much as possible.
2. Pour water to a depth of 2 inches in the bottom of a large saucepan.
3. Add garlic, lemon slice and salt, then bring to a boil.
4. Place the artichokes in the boiling water, cover tightly and cook over medium heat about 40 minutes or until the stems can be easily pierced with a fork.
5. Remove the artichokes from the water and place upside down to drain until cool enough to handle easily. Remove the center leaves and spread the artichoke open very carefully. Reach down into the center and remove the furry choke, pulling it out a little at a time.
6. Place right side up in a glass baking dish.
7. Pour a little French Dressing into each artichoke and allow to stand several hours in the refrigerator.
8. Place the marinated artichoke bowl on a plate and with a paper towel blot out excessive dressing. Fill with Consommé Madrilene and top with 1 tablespoon of sour cream and 1/2 teaspoon caviar. On the side, heap a little sour cream as a dip for the leaves. Thus you eat your soup out of your artichoke bowl and then you eat the bowl for your salad. Makes 10 servings.

COMSOMMÉ MADRILENE

3 large, ripe tomatoes, sliced
2 stalks celery (tops removed), chopped
1 leek, white part only, chopped
1 carrot, sliced
1 onion, sliced
1 teaspoon lemon juice
6 peppercorns
2 quarts (8 cups) chicken stock
2 bay leaves
2 envelopes (2 scant tablespoons) unflavored gelatin
1/4 cup cold water
Salt and freshly ground black pepper

1. In a large pot or soup kettle place all ingredients except the gelatin, cold water, salt and pepper.
2. Cover, leaving the lid ajar about 1 inch to allow the steam to escape. Simmer for 2 hours.
3. Soften gelatin in 1/4 cup water and add to the hot consommé. Stir until completely dissolved.
4. Cool slightly and strain through a fine strainer. Season to taste with salt and pepper.

5. Cool to room temperature and refrigerate. When completely jelled, unmold and cut off the part containing the sediment. Cut up the clear part and serve in sherbet glasses or cups—or artichoke bowls! Makes 10 servings.

FRENCH DRESSING

1-1/2 tablespoons red wine vinegar
1 teaspoon lemon juice
1/4 teaspoon dry mustard
1/4 teaspoon salt
1 tablespoon water
5 tablespoons corn oil
Dash freshly ground black pepper
1/8 teaspoon dried basil or tarragon (optional)

1. Mix the vinegar, lemon juice, mustard and salt until the salt is dissolved.
2. Add the water. Slowly add the oil and mix thoroughly.
3. Add the pepper and basil and pour the dressing into a jar with a tightly fitted lid. Shake vigorously for 30 seconds.
4. Store in the refrigerator. Makes 1/2 cup.

MYSTERY PILAF

1/2 cup uncooked vermicelli, broken in 1-inch pieces
3 tablespoons corn oil
1 cup long-grain white rice
1/2 medium-size onion, thinly sliced
2 cups chicken stock
2 tablespoons soy sauce
1 teaspoons dried thyme

1. Put the vermicelli on a cookie sheet with sides or in a baking dish. Place in a 400° oven and stir occasionally until a rich brown in color.
2. Heat the oil in a cured heavy iron skillet and add the rice and onion slices to the heated oil. Cook, stirring frequently, until browned thoroughly.
3. Add the browned vermicelli, soy sauce and thyme to the chicken stock and bring to the boiling point.
4. Put the rice mixture in a casserole dish with a tight-fitting lid and add the hot stock. Stir and cover. Place in a 400° oven for 40 minutes.
5. Remove from the oven and allow to stand for 10 minutes before removing the lid.
6. To reheat: Add 2 or 3 tablespoons of chicken stock to the cold rice and mix thoroughly. Cover and heat slowly in a 300° oven for 15 minutes.
Makes 10 servings.

TARRAGON BAKED TOMATOES

5 small tomatoes
2/3 cup buttermilk
1/2 cup grated Parmesan cheese
1 teaspoon dried tarragon, crushed
Freshly ground black pepper

1. Cut the tomatoes in half and remove the seeds.
2. Divide the buttermilk evenly into each tomato half.
3. Combine the grated cheese and crushed tarragon and mix well. Sprinkle the cheese-tarragon mixture evenly over the tops of the tomatoes.
4. Sprinkle the top of each tomato lightly with freshly ground black pepper.
5. Put the tomatoes in a 400° oven for 15 minutes. Then put them under the broiler until lightly browned.
Makes 10 servings.

COQ AU VIN

5 whole chicken breasts
1/4 cup butter or corn-oil margarine
2 garlic buds, minced
Salt and freshly ground black pepper
20 small boiling onions, peeled
20 large fresh mushrooms
1 quart (4 cups) beef stock
1 tablespoon finely chopped shallots
1/2 cup burgundy
1/4 cup sherry
1/4 cup dry white wine (I prefer chablis)
4 tablespoons cornstarch
1/4 cup cold water
1/2 teaspoon salt

Dash of freshly ground black pepper
2 teaspoons Kitchen Bouquet

1. Bone, skin and then halve the chicken breasts; remove all visible fat.
2. Melt butter or margarine in a large cured iron skillet. Add the garlic and cook a few minutes.
3. Salt and pepper both sides of the chicken breasts. Put the chicken in the skillet and cook until a rich deep brown on one side.
4. While the chicken is browning, put the onions in a large saucepan with lightly salted water and gently boil, covered, about 12 minutes, or until fork tender.
5. Carefully wash the mushrooms and remove the stems.
6. When the chicken is browned on one side, turn over chicken, add the mushroom caps and cook with the chicken until the other side is also brown. Put the chicken and mushrooms in a flat baking dish.
7. Drain the onions and add them to the chicken.
8. In a saucepan, heat the beef stock. In another large pan, combine the chopped shallots and wines and heat over fairly high heat, boiling it until the liquid has reduced in volume by one-third. When reduced, add the heated beef stock to the wine and then lower the heat to medium.
9. Allow the mixture to come again to a simmering boil. Mix the cornstarch and water until completely dissolved. Add the cornstarch mixture to the sauce, mixing thoroughly with a wire whisk.
10. Season to taste with salt and pepper. To get the rich dark brown color associated with the classic French brown sauce, add the Kitchen Bouquet.
11. Pour the brown sauce over the chicken, and place, uncovered, in a 350° oven for 30 minutes.

You can make this dish in the morning up to the point where it goes in the oven. Then put it in the refrigerator until dinner time. Take it out at least 1 hour before you plan to put it in the oven.
Makes 10 servings.

CRÊPES SUZETTE

2 cups non-fat milk
1-1/2 cups all-purpose flour
1/2 teaspoon salt
4 eggs, lightly beaten
2 teaspoons butter or
   corn-oil margarine
2 cups fresh orange juice
4 teaspoons cornstarch
1/4 cup fructose
2 tablespoons freshly
   grated orange peel (be
   careful to use only the
   colored part of the peel)
1/2 cup orange liqueur
2 tablespoons corn-oil
   margarine
2 tablespoons additional
   fructose
1/4 cup brandy (optional)

1. Put the milk, flour and salt in a bowl and beat with an egg beater until well mixed. Beat in the eggs and mix well.
2. In a cured iron omelet or crêpe pan, melt the butter or margarine. When the butter is melted and the pan is hot, tilt the pan to make sure the entire surface is buttered.
3. Pour in just enough crêpe batter to cover barely the bottom of the pan (about 2 tablespoons) and tilt the pan from side to side to spread the batter evenly. When the edges start to curl, carefully turn the crêpe with a spatula and brown the other side.
4. To keep the crêpes pliable, put them in a covered casserole in a warm oven as you make them. They may be made well ahead of time. To store, separate them with wax paper or aluminum foil, cover tightly and refrigerate. Then before using them, warm them in a low oven.
5. Pour the orange juice in a chafing dish pan. Add the cornstarch and fructose to the juice. Stir until the cornstarch is dissolved.
6. Slowly bring the mixture to a boil and simmer, stirring constantly with a wire whisk until slightly thickened.
7. Remove the pan from the heat. Add the grated orange peel, orange liqueur and corn-oil margarine. Stir until the margarine is completely melted.
8. Return the pan to the heat. Dip both sides of each crêpe in the sauce and fold it in half and then in half again, forming a triangle, and put it on a plate or serving platter. Continue until all the crêpes have been dipped and folded and arranged on the serving dish.
9. Sprinkle the additional fructose evenly over the crêpes.
10. At this point if you wish you can add the brandy to the remaining sauce and ignite it with a lighted match, shaking the chafing dish gently back and forth while spooning the flaming liquid over the folded crêpes until the flame goes out. If you plan to flame your Crêpes Suzette, do it carefully — so you do not burn yourself.
Makes 10 servings
(20 crêpes)

Guests

Accept ✔
Refuse ✗

Seating Chart

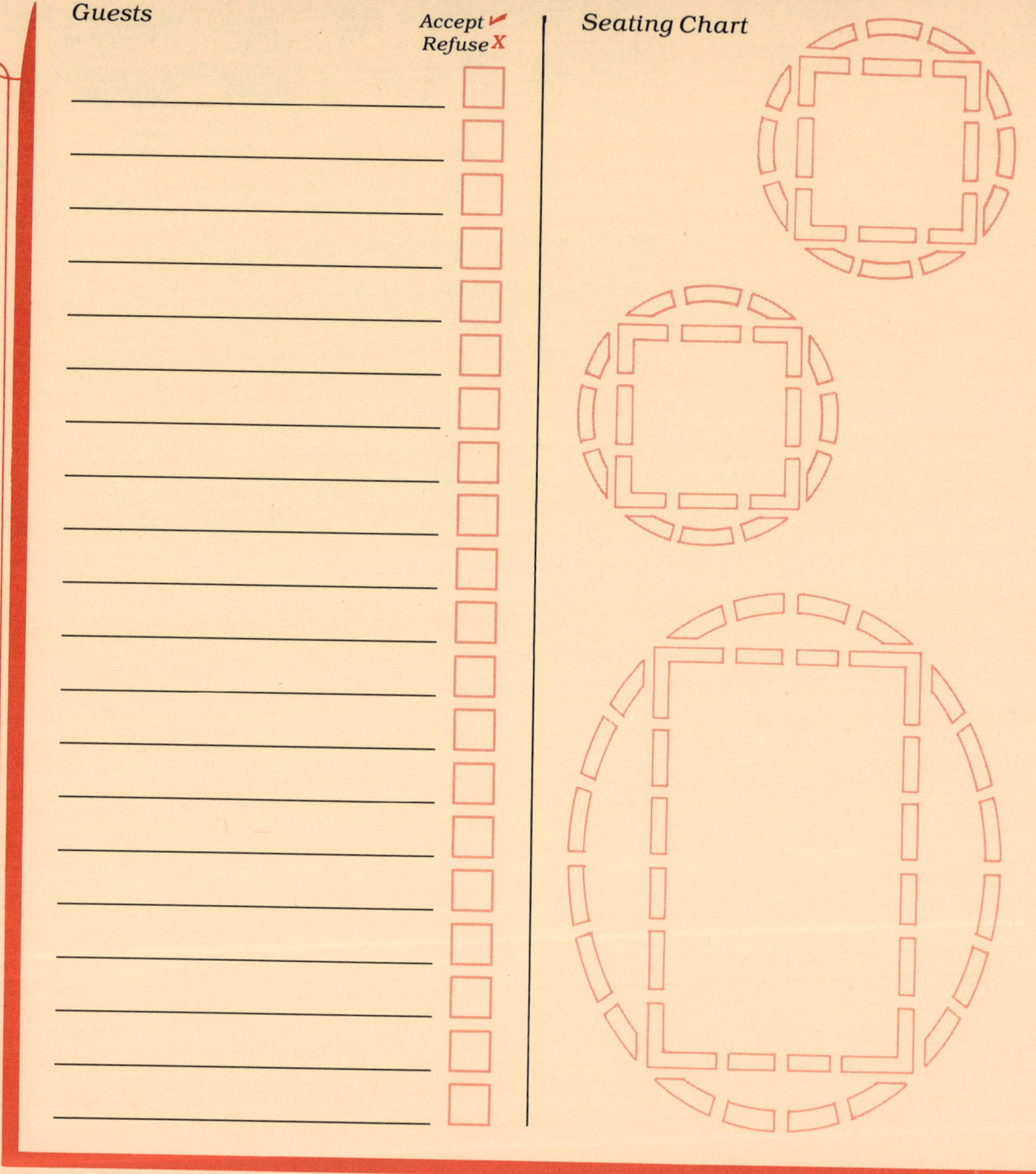

Occasion _____

Place _____

Day _____

Date _____ Time _____

Checklist:

- [ ] Invitations _____
- [ ] Reminders _____
- [ ] Menu _____
- [ ] Table Linens _____
- [ ] China _____
  _____
- [ ] Crystal _____
- [ ] Silver _____
  _____
- [ ] Serving Pieces _____
  _____
- [ ] Flowers _____
- [ ] Table Decorations _____
  _____
- [ ] Candles _____
- [ ] Place Cards _____
- [ ] Favors _____
  _____
- [ ] Shopping List _____

Rentals _____
_____

Help _____
_____

Costs:	Budgeted	Actual
Food	_____	_____
Wine	_____	_____
Liquor	_____	_____
Flowers	_____	_____
Rentals	_____	_____
Help	_____	_____
Other	_____	_____

Menu

Wines: _____

_____

Liquor and Liqueurs: _____

_____

Dress:
  Hostess _____
  Host _____
_____

Review: _____

_____

Guests

Seating Chart

Accept ✔
Refuse X

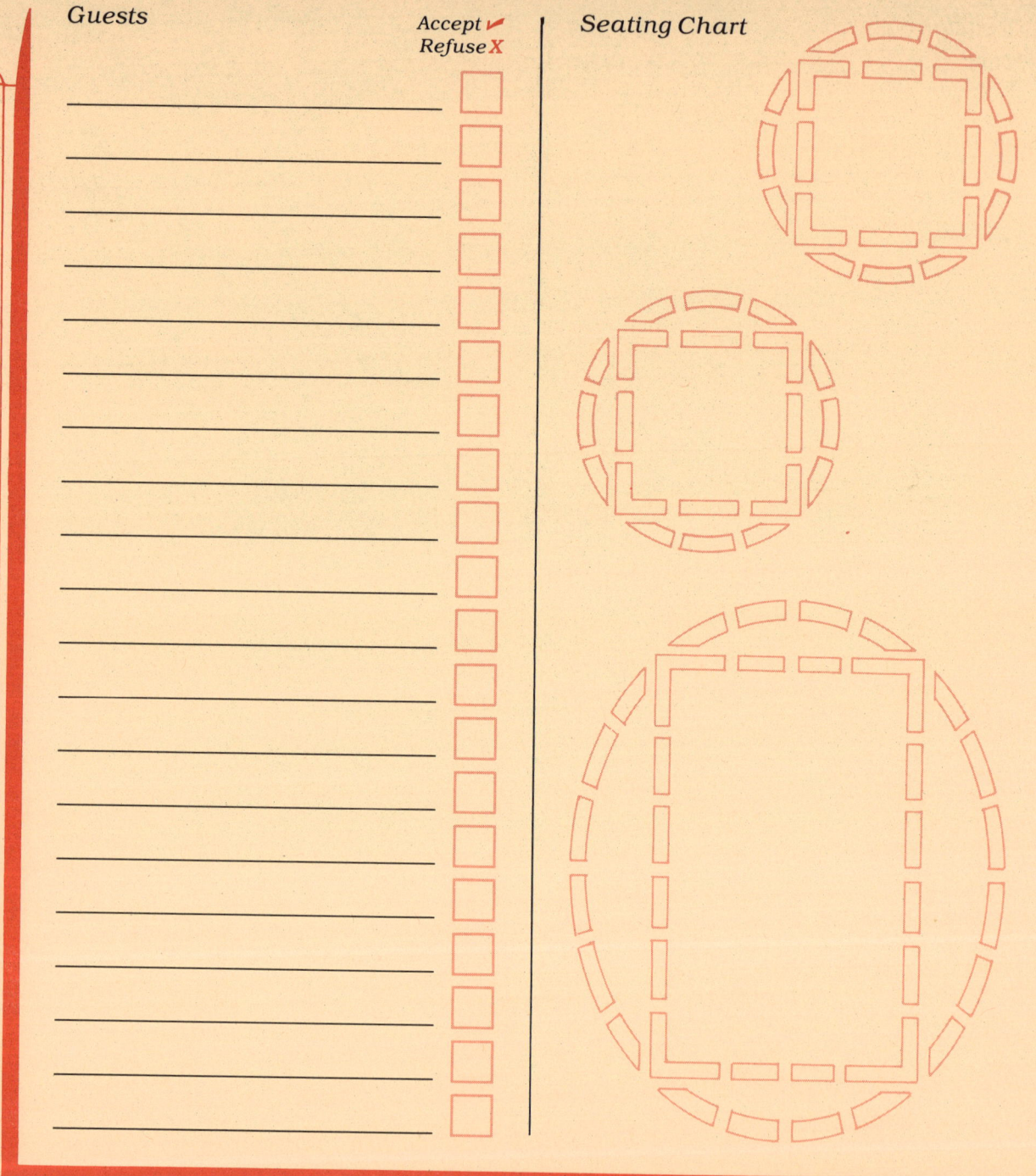

Occasion _____

Place _____

Day _____

Date _____ Time _____

Checklist:

☐ Invitations _____
☐ Reminders _____
☐ Menu _____
☐ Table Linens _____
☐ China _____
_____
☐ Crystal _____
☐ Silver _____
_____
☐ Serving Pieces _____
_____
☐ Flowers _____
☐ Table Decorations _____
_____
☐ Candles _____
☐ Place Cards _____
☐ Favors _____
_____
☐ Shopping List _____

Rentals _____
_____

Help _____
_____

Costs:	Budgeted	Actual
Food	_____	_____
Wine	_____	_____
Liquor	_____	_____
Flowers	_____	_____
Rentals	_____	_____
Help	_____	_____
Other	_____	_____

Menu

Wines:

_____

Liquor and Liqueurs:

_____

Dress:
   Hostess _____
   Host _____

Review:

_____

Guests

Seating Chart

Accept ✔
Refuse ✗

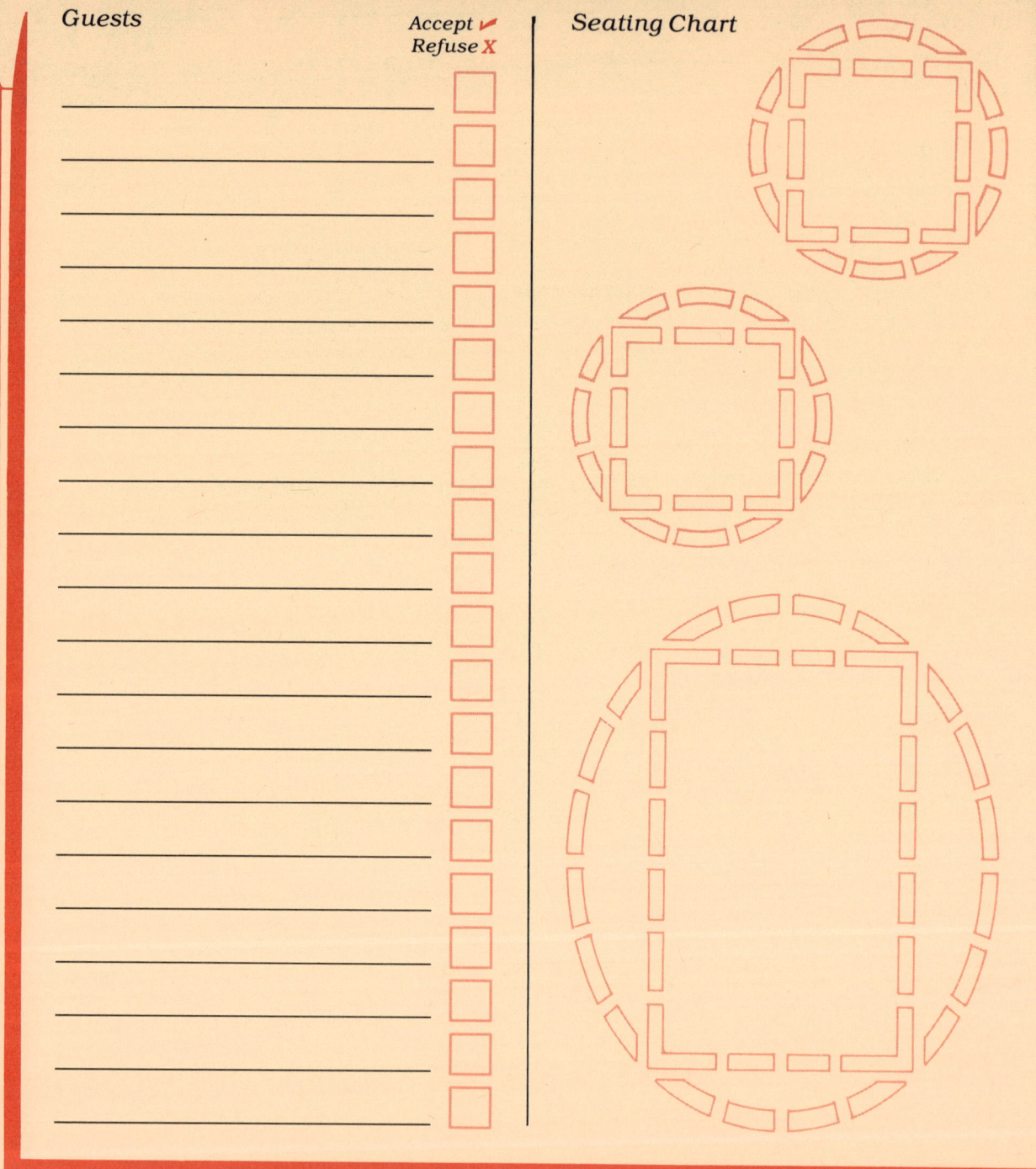

Occasion _____

Place _____

Day _____

Date _____ Time _____

Checklist:

☐ Invitations _____

☐ Reminders _____

☐ Menu _____

☐ Table Linens _____

☐ China _____

☐ Crystal _____

☐ Silver _____

☐ Serving Pieces _____

☐ Flowers _____

☐ Table Decorations _____

☐ Candles _____

☐ Place Cards _____

☐ Favors _____

☐ Shopping List _____

Rentals _____

Help _____

Costs:	Budgeted	Actual
Food	_____	_____
Wine	_____	_____
Liquor	_____	_____
Flowers	_____	_____
Rentals	_____	_____
Help	_____	_____
Other	_____	_____

Menu

Wines:

Liquor and Liqueurs:

Dress:
   Hostess _____
   Host _____

Review:

Guests

Accept ✔
Refuse ✗

Seating Chart

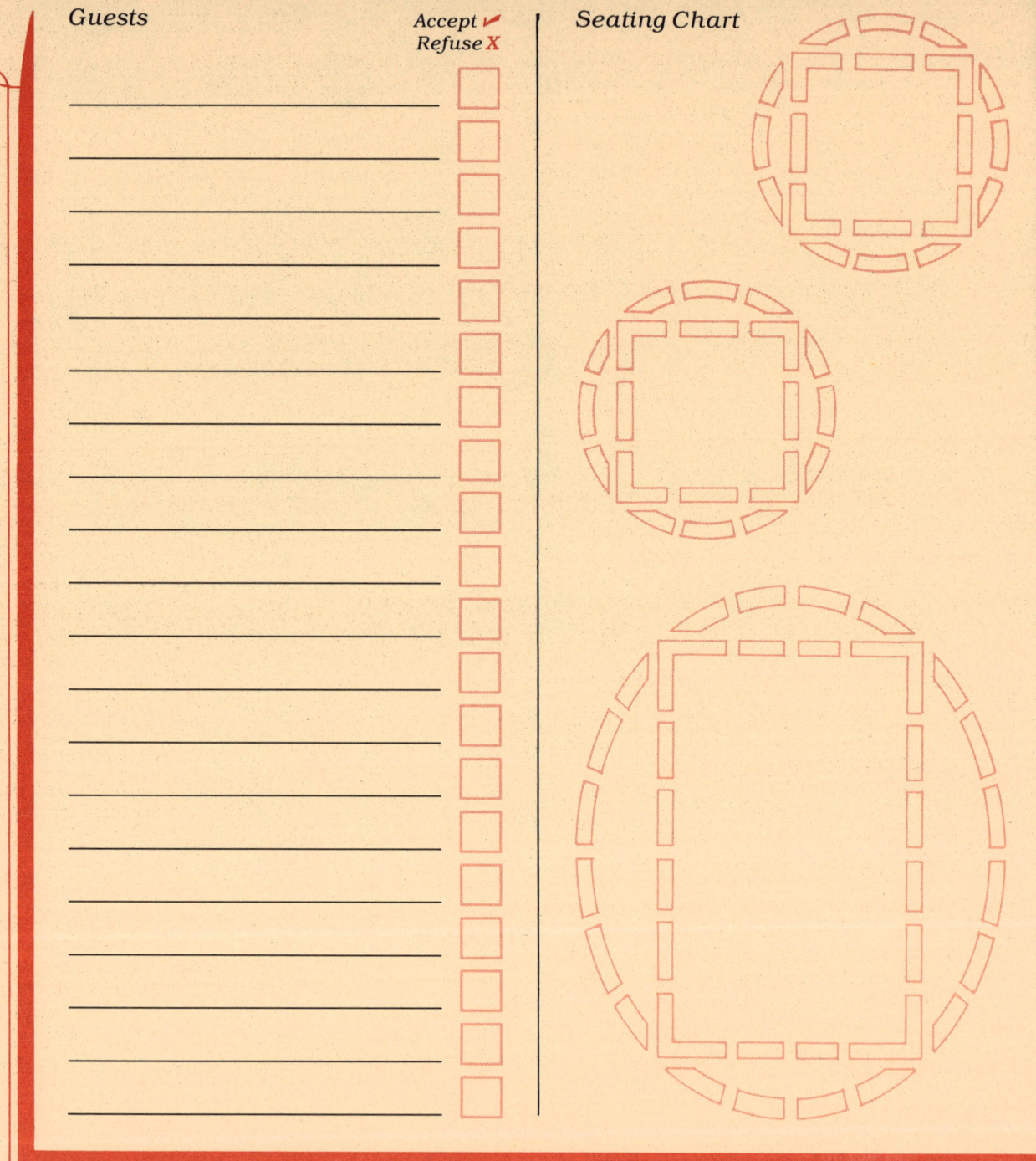

Occasion _____

Place _____

Day _____

Date _____ Time _____

Checklist:

☐ Invitations _____

☐ Reminders _____

☐ Menu _____

☐ Table Linens _____

☐ China _____

_____

☐ Crystal _____

☐ Silver _____

_____

☐ Serving Pieces _____

_____

☐ Flowers _____

☐ Table Decorations _____

_____

☐ Candles _____

☐ Place Cards _____

☐ Favors _____

_____

☐ Shopping List _____

Rentals _____

_____

Help _____

_____

Costs:	Budgeted	Actual
Food	_____	_____
Wine	_____	_____
Liquor	_____	_____
Flowers	_____	_____
Rentals	_____	_____
Help	_____	_____
Other	_____	_____

Menu

Wines:

_____

Liquor and Liqueurs:

_____

Dress:

Hostess _____

Host _____

_____

Review:

_____

Guests

Accept ✔
Refuse X

Seating Chart

Occasion _____

Place _____

Day _____

Date _____ Time _____

Checklist:

☐ Invitations _____
☐ Reminders _____
☐ Menu _____
☐ Table Linens _____
☐ China _____
 _____
☐ Crystal _____
☐ Silver _____
 _____
☐ Serving Pieces _____
 _____
☐ Flowers _____
☐ Table Decorations _____
 _____
☐ Candles _____
☐ Place Cards _____
☐ Favors _____
 _____
☐ Shopping List _____

Rentals _____
_____

Help _____
_____

Costs:	Budgeted	Actual
Food	_____	_____
Wine	_____	_____
Liquor	_____	_____
Flowers	_____	_____
Rentals	_____	_____
Help	_____	_____
Other	_____	_____

Menu

Wines:
_____

Liquor and Liqueurs:
_____

Dress:
 Hostess _____
 Host _____

Review:

_____

Guests

Seating Chart

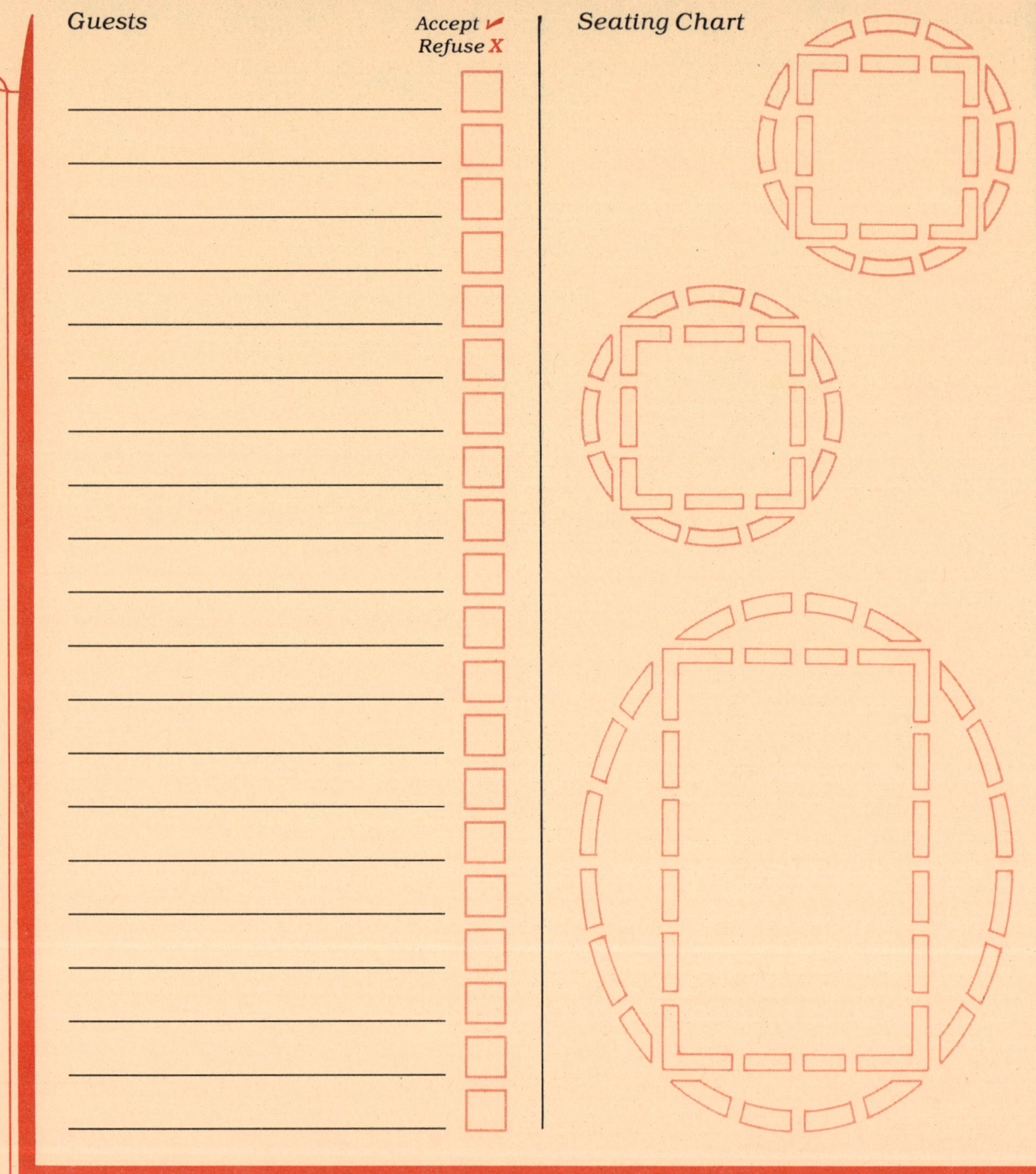

Occasion _____

Place _____

Day _____

Date _____ Time _____

Checklist:

☐ Invitations _____

☐ Reminders _____

☐ Menu _____

☐ Table Linens _____

☐ China _____

_____

☐ Crystal _____

☐ Silver _____

_____

☐ Serving Pieces _____

_____

☐ Flowers _____

☐ Table Decorations _____

_____

☐ Candles _____

☐ Place Cards _____

☐ Favors _____

_____

☐ Shopping List _____

Rentals _____

_____

Help _____

Costs:	Budgeted	Actual
Food		
Wine	_____	_____
Liquor	_____	_____
Flowers	_____	_____
Rentals	_____	_____
Help	_____	_____
Other	_____	_____

Menu

Wines:

_____

Liquor and Liqueurs:

_____

Dress:
  Hostess _____
  Host _____

_____

Review:

_____

Guests

Seating Chart

Accept ✔
Refuse **X**

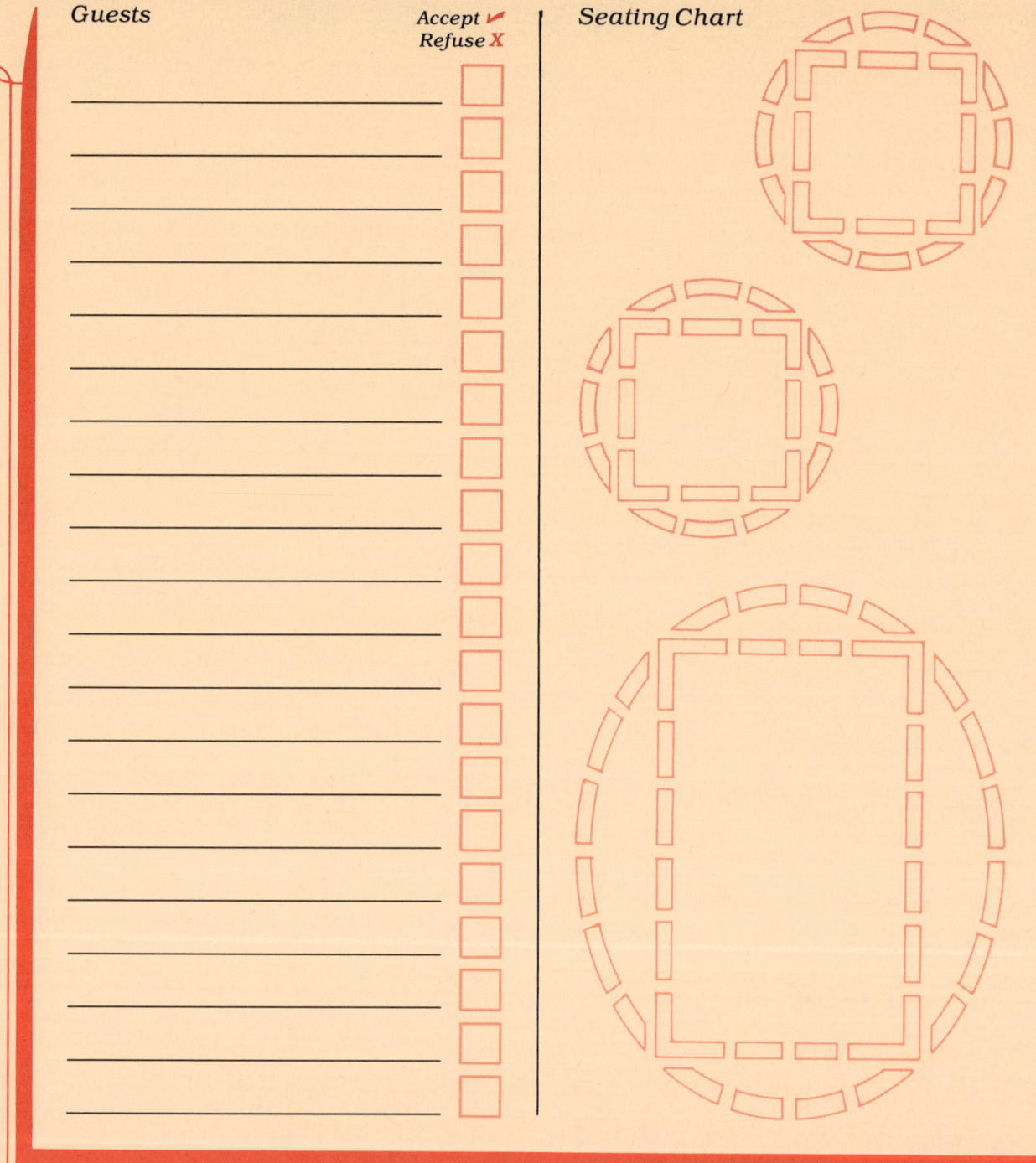

Occasion _____

Place _____

Day _____

Date _____Time _____

Checklist:

☐ Invitations _____
☐ Reminders _____
☐ Menu _____
☐ Table Linens _____
☐ China _____
   _____
☐ Crystal _____
☐ Silver _____
   _____
☐ Serving Pieces _____
   _____
☐ Flowers _____
☐ Table Decorations _____
   _____
☐ Candles _____
☐ Place Cards _____
☐ Favors _____
   _____
☐ Shopping List _____

Rentals _____
   _____

Help _____

Costs:	Budgeted	Actual
Food	_____	_____
Wine	_____	_____
Liquor	_____	_____
Flowers	_____	_____
Rentals	_____	_____
Help	_____	_____
Other	_____	_____

Menu

Wines:

_____

Liquor and Liqueurs:

_____

Dress:
   Hostess _____
   Host _____

Review:

_____

Guests

Seating Chart

Accept ✔
Refuse ✗

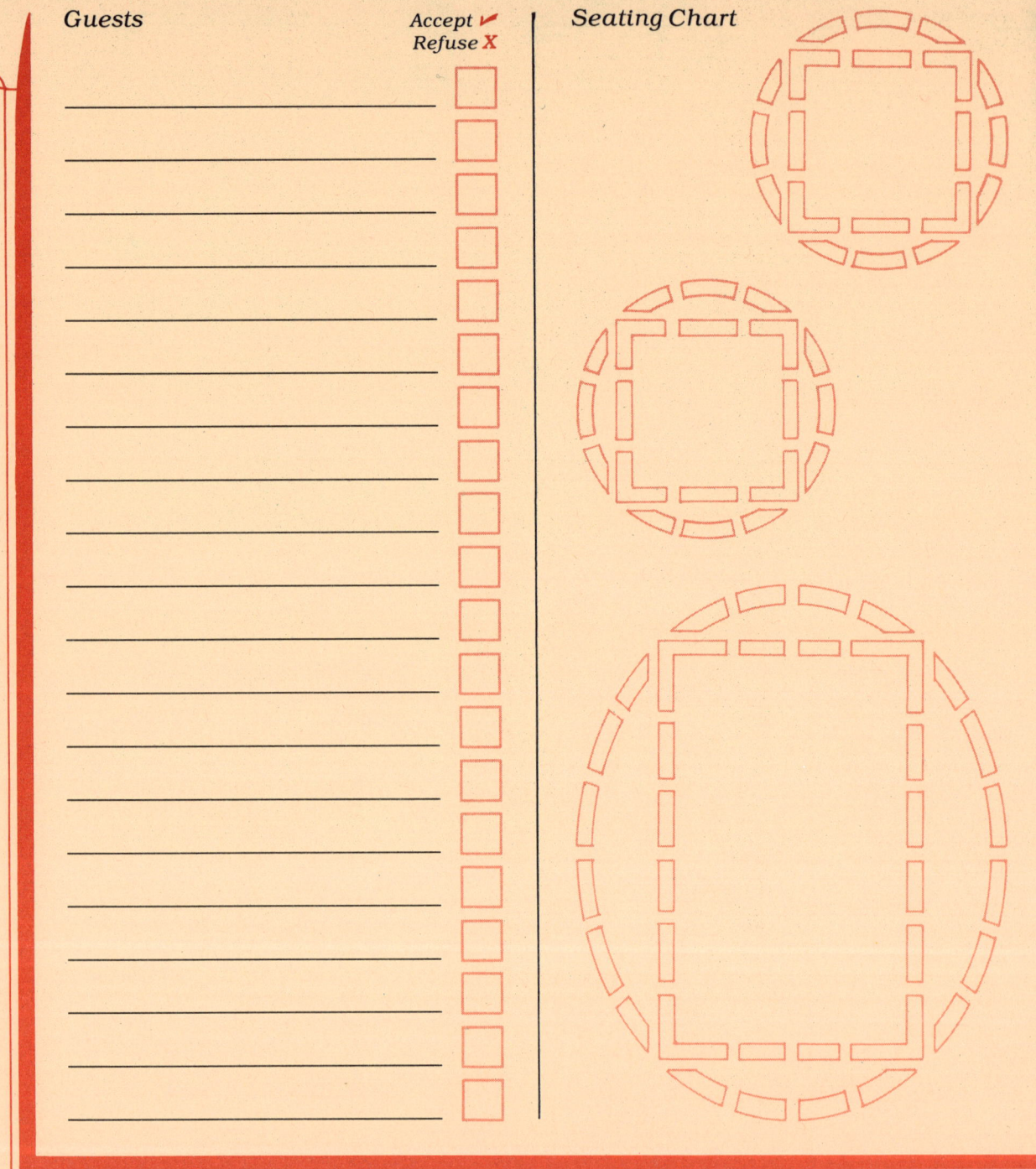

Occasion _____

Place _____

Day _____

Date _____ Time _____

Checklist:

☐ Invitations _____

☐ Reminders _____

☐ Menu _____

☐ Table Linens _____

☐ China _____

   _____

☐ Crystal _____

☐ Silver _____

   _____

☐ Serving Pieces _____

   _____

☐ Flowers _____

☐ Table Decorations _____

   _____

☐ Candles _____

☐ Place Cards _____

☐ Favors _____

   _____

☐ Shopping List _____

Rentals _____

_____

Help _____

_____

Costs:	Budgeted	Actual
Food	_____	_____
Wine	_____	_____
Liquor	_____	_____
Flowers	_____	_____
Rentals	_____	_____
Help	_____	_____
Other	_____	_____

Menu

Wines:

_____

Liquor and Liqueurs:

_____

Dress:

  Hostess _____

  Host _____

_____

Review:

_____

Guests

Seating Chart

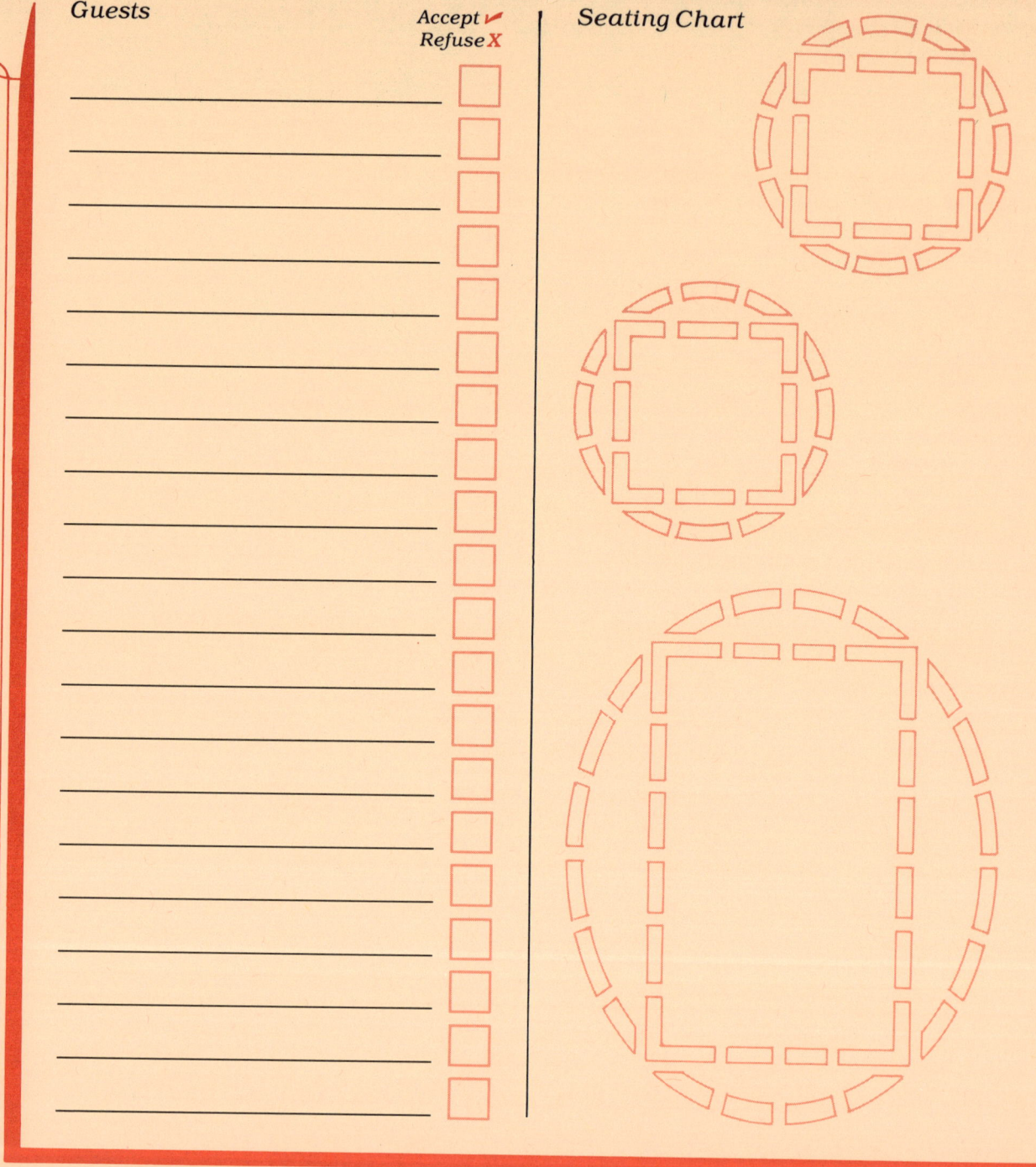

Occasion _____

Place _____

Day _____

Date _____ Time _____

Checklist:

- ☐ Invitations _____
- ☐ Reminders _____
- ☐ Menu _____
- ☐ Table Linens _____
- ☐ China _____
  _____
- ☐ Crystal _____
- ☐ Silver _____
  _____
- ☐ Serving Pieces _____
  _____
- ☐ Flowers _____
- ☐ Table Decorations _____
  _____
- ☐ Candles _____
- ☐ Place Cards _____
- ☐ Favors _____
  _____
- ☐ Shopping List _____

Rentals _____
_____

Help _____

Costs:	Budgeted	Actual
Food	_____	_____
Wine	_____	_____
Liquor	_____	_____
Flowers	_____	_____
Rentals	_____	_____
Help	_____	_____
Other	_____	_____

Menu

Wines:

_____

Liquor and Liqueurs:

_____

Dress:
Hostess _____
Host _____

Review:

_____

Guests

Accept ✔
Refuse ✗

Seating Chart

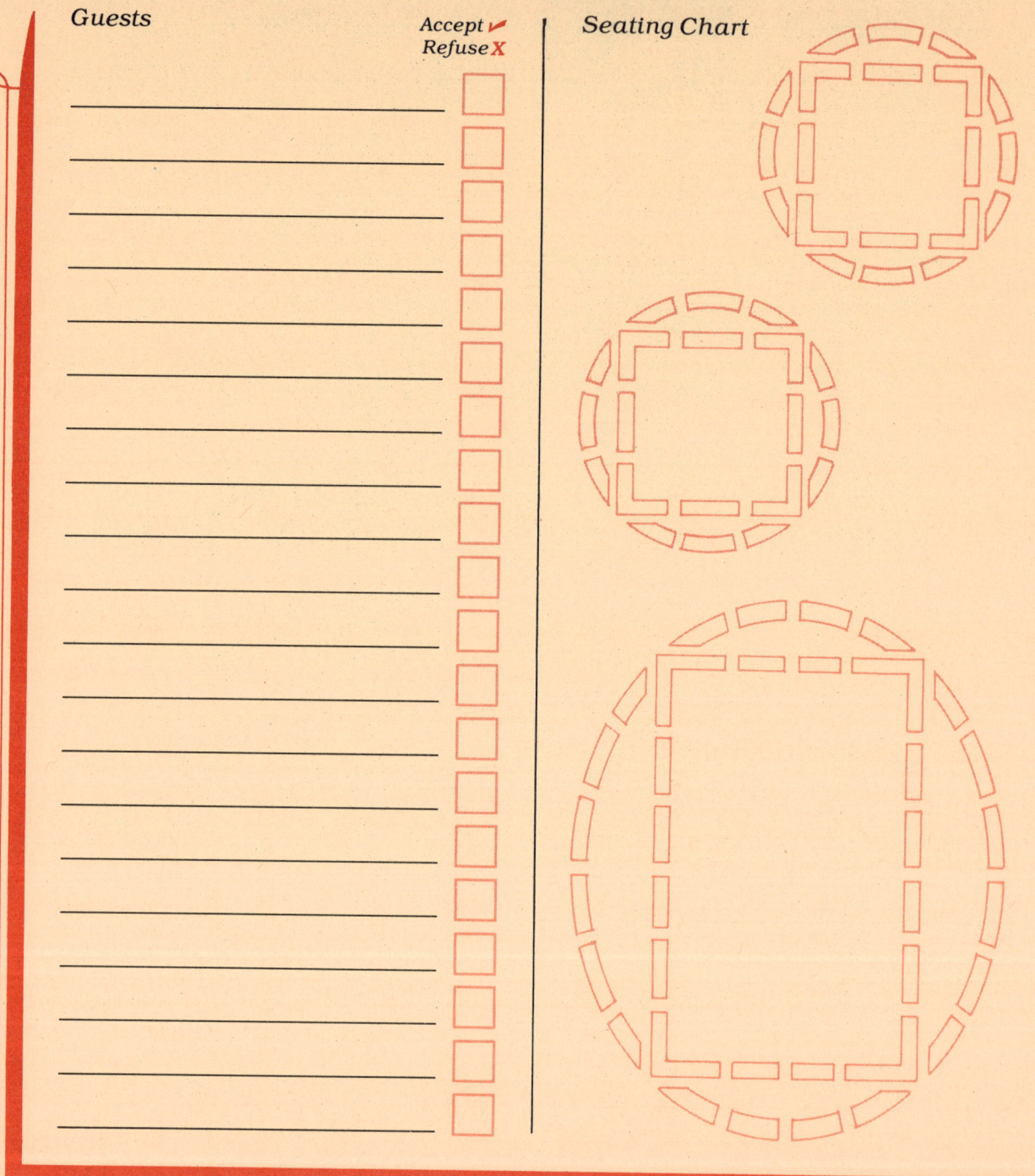

Occasion _____

Place _____

Day _____

Date _____ Time _____

Checklist:

☐ Invitations _____

☐ Reminders _____

☐ Menu _____

☐ Table Linens _____

☐ China _____

_____

☐ Crystal _____

☐ Silver _____

_____

☐ Serving Pieces _____

_____

☐ Flowers _____

☐ Table Decorations _____

_____

☐ Candles _____

☐ Place Cards _____

☐ Favors _____

_____

☐ Shopping List _____

Rentals _____

_____

Help _____

_____

Costs:	Budgeted	Actual
Food	_____	_____
Wine	_____	_____
Liquor	_____	_____
Flowers	_____	_____
Rentals	_____	_____
Help	_____	_____
Other	_____	_____

Menu

Wines:

_____

Liquor and Liqueurs:

_____

Dress:
Hostess _____
Host _____

_____

Review:

_____

Guests

Seating Chart

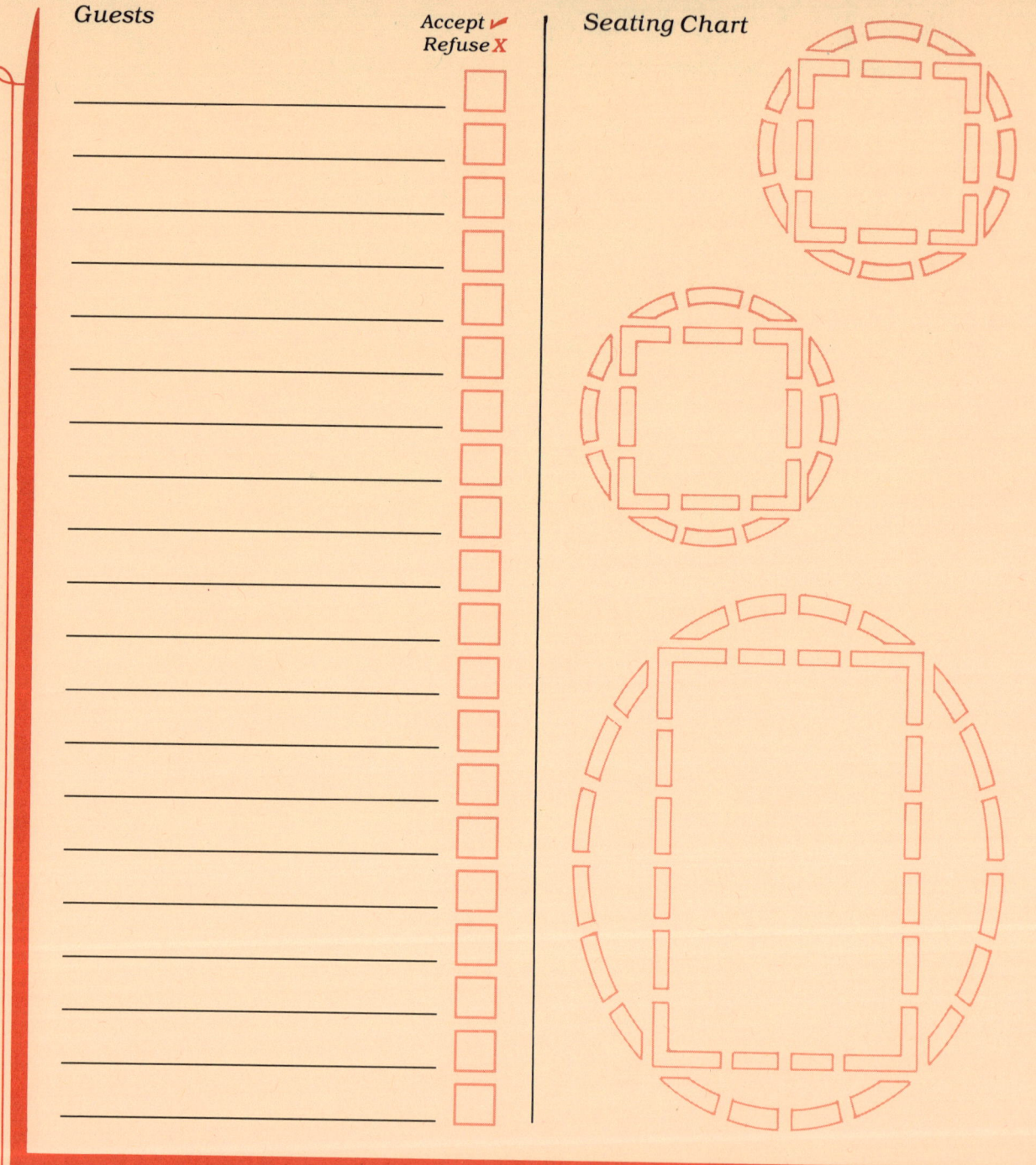

Occasion _____

Place _____

Day _____

Date _____ Time _____

Checklist:

- ☐ Invitations _____
- ☐ Reminders _____
- ☐ Menu _____
- ☐ Table Linens _____
- ☐ China _____
  _____
- ☐ Crystal _____
- ☐ Silver _____
  _____
- ☐ Serving Pieces _____
  _____
- ☐ Flowers _____
- ☐ Table Decorations _____
  _____
- ☐ Candles _____
- ☐ Place Cards _____
- ☐ Favors _____
  _____
- ☐ Shopping List _____

Rentals _____
_____

Help _____
_____

Costs:	Budgeted	Actual
Food	_____	_____
Wine	_____	_____
Liquor	_____	_____
Flowers	_____	_____
Rentals	_____	_____
Help	_____	_____
Other	_____	_____

Menu

Wines:

_____

Liquor and Liqueurs:

_____

Dress:
Hostess _____
Host _____
_____

Review:

_____

Guests

Seating Chart

| | Accept ✔ |
| | Refuse ✗ |

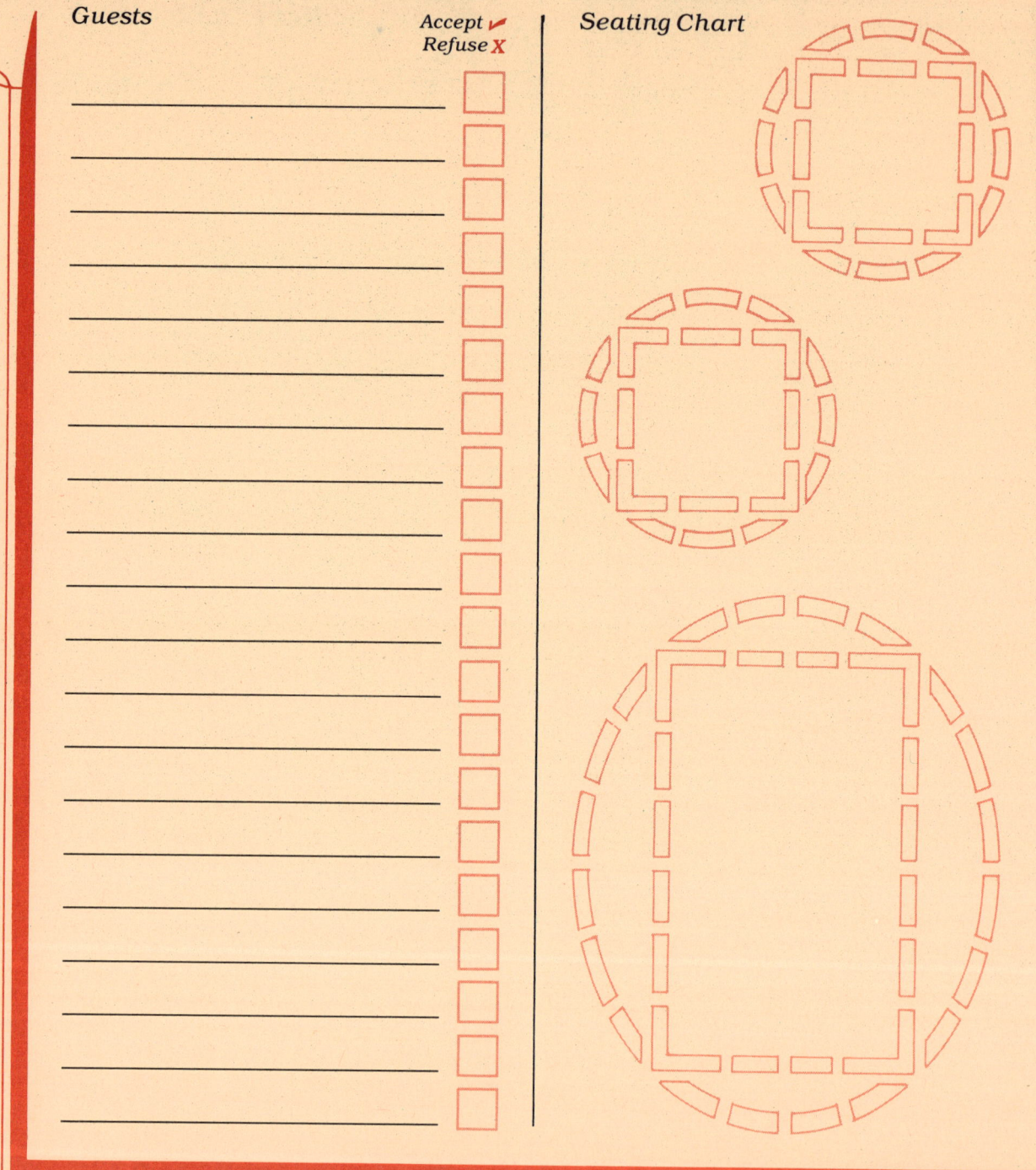

Occasion _____

Place _____

Day _____

Date _____ Time _____

Checklist:

☐ Invitations _____
☐ Reminders _____
☐ Menu _____
☐ Table Linens _____
☐ China _____
_____
☐ Crystal _____
☐ Silver _____
_____
☐ Serving Pieces _____
_____
☐ Flowers _____
☐ Table Decorations _____
_____
☐ Candles _____
☐ Place Cards _____
☐ Favors _____
_____
☐ Shopping List _____

Rentals _____
_____

Help _____
_____

Costs:	Budgeted	Actual
Food	_____	_____
Wine	_____	_____
Liquor	_____	_____
Flowers	_____	_____
Rentals	_____	_____
Help	_____	_____
Other	_____	_____

Menu

Wines:

_____

Liquor and Liqueurs:

_____

Dress:
Hostess _____
Host _____

Review:

_____

Guests

Accept ✔
Refuse ✗

Seating Chart

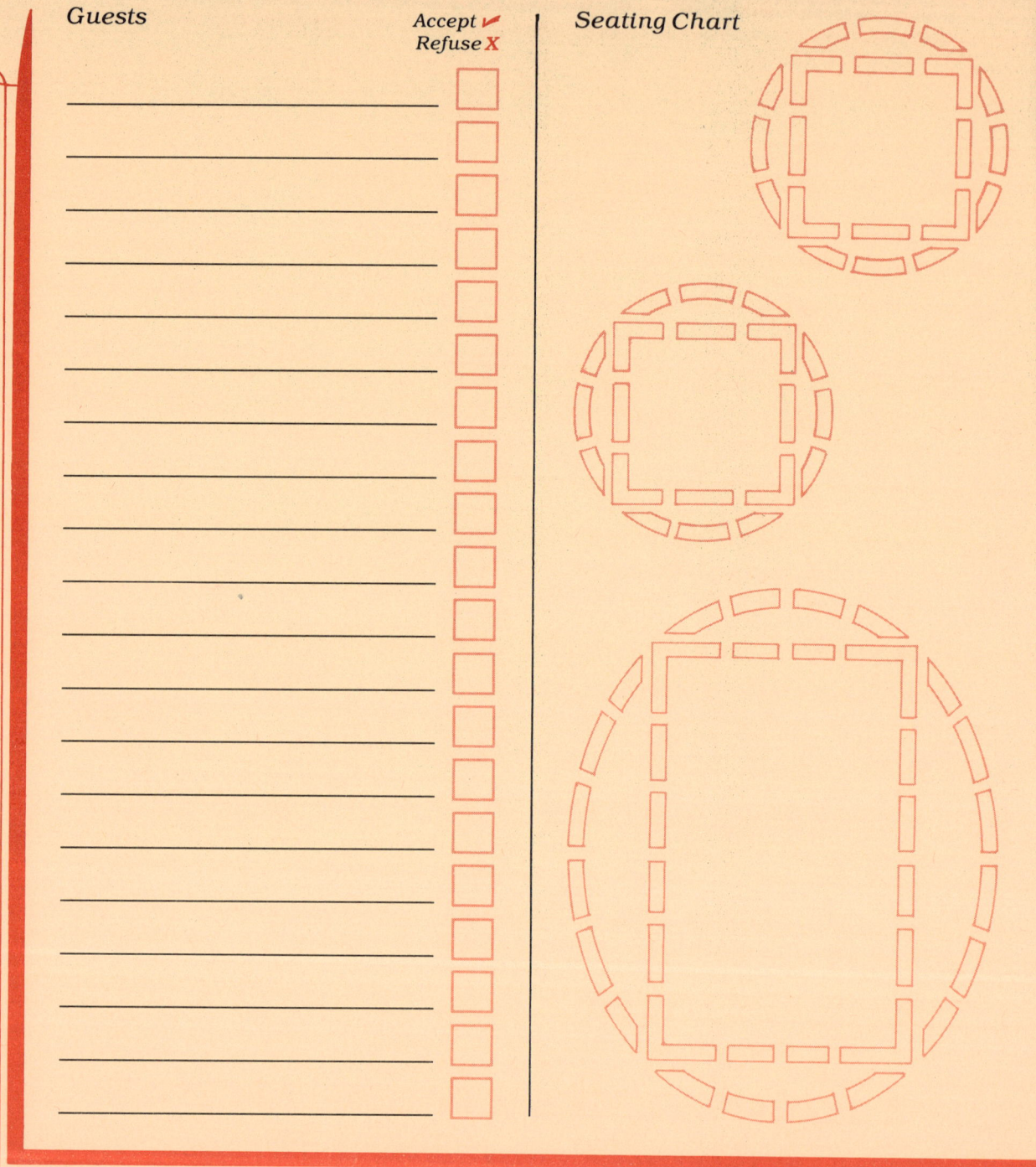

Occasion _____

Place _____

Day _____

Date _____ Time _____

Checklist:

- ☐ Invitations _____
- ☐ Reminders _____
- ☐ Menu _____
- ☐ Table Linens _____
- ☐ China _____
  _____
- ☐ Crystal _____
- ☐ Silver _____
  _____
- ☐ Serving Pieces _____
  _____
- ☐ Flowers _____
- ☐ Table Decorations _____
  _____
- ☐ Candles _____
- ☐ Place Cards _____
- ☐ Favors _____
  _____
- ☐ Shopping List _____

Rentals _____
_____

Help _____

Costs:	Budgeted	Actual
Food	_____	_____
Wine	_____	_____
Liquor	_____	_____
Flowers	_____	_____
Rentals	_____	_____
Help	_____	_____
Other	_____	_____

Menu

Wines:

_____

Liquor and Liqueurs:

_____

Dress:
   Hostess _____
   Host _____

Review:

_____

Guests

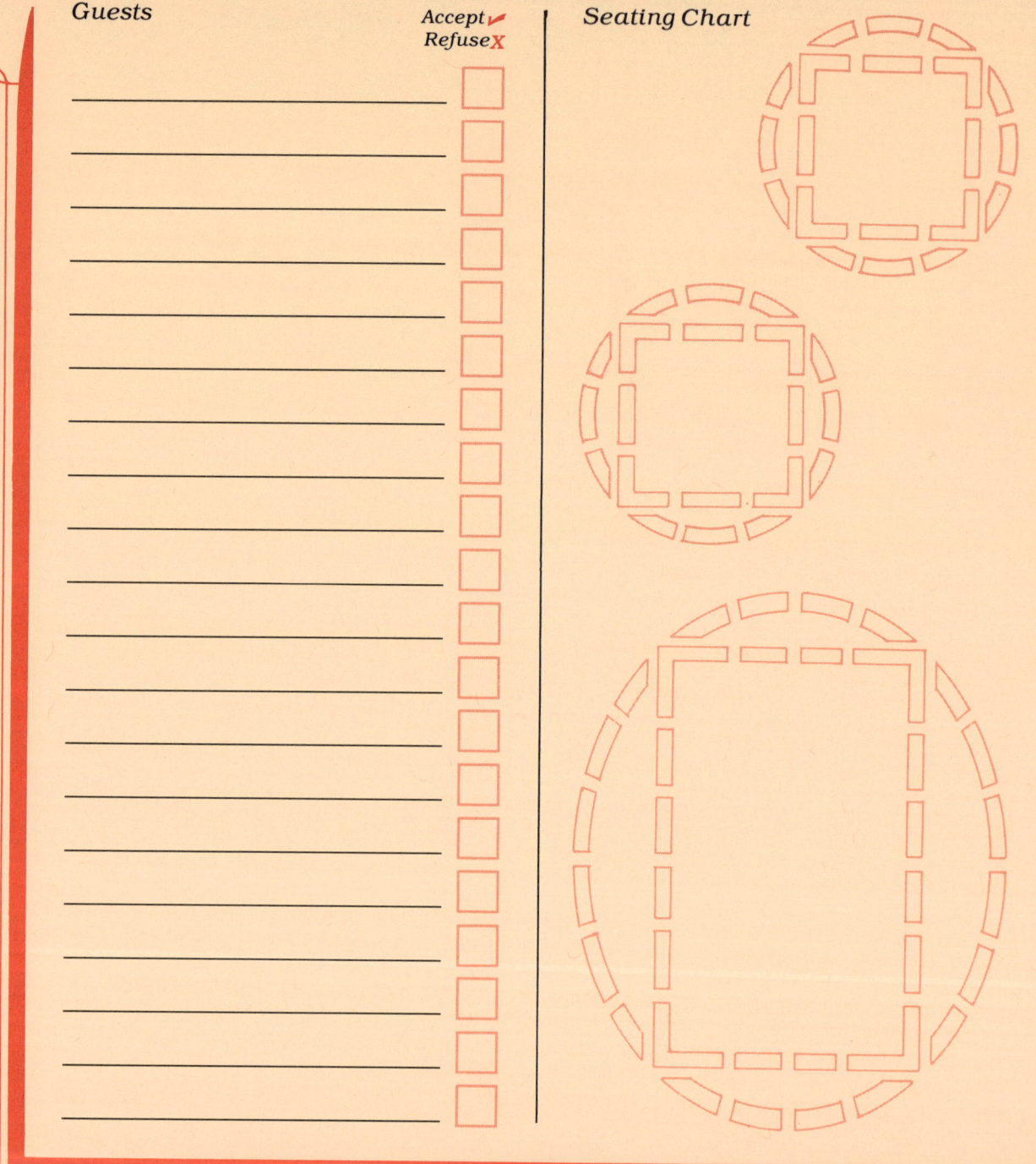

Accept ✔
Refuse **X**

Seating Chart

Occasion _____

Place _____

Day _____

Date _____ Time _____

Checklist:

☐ Invitations _____

☐ Reminders _____

☐ Menu _____

☐ Table Linens _____

☐ China _____

_____

☐ Crystal _____

☐ Silver _____

_____

☐ Serving Pieces _____

_____

☐ Flowers _____

☐ Table Decorations _____

_____

☐ Candles _____

☐ Place Cards _____

☐ Favors _____

_____

☐ Shopping List _____

Rentals _____

_____

Help _____

Costs:	Budgeted	Actual
Food	_____	_____
Wine	_____	_____
Liquor	_____	_____
Flowers	_____	_____
Rentals	_____	_____
Help	_____	_____
Other	_____	_____

Menu

Wines:

_____

Liquor and Liqueurs:

_____

Dress:
  Hostess _____
  Host _____

Review:

_____

Guests

Seating Chart

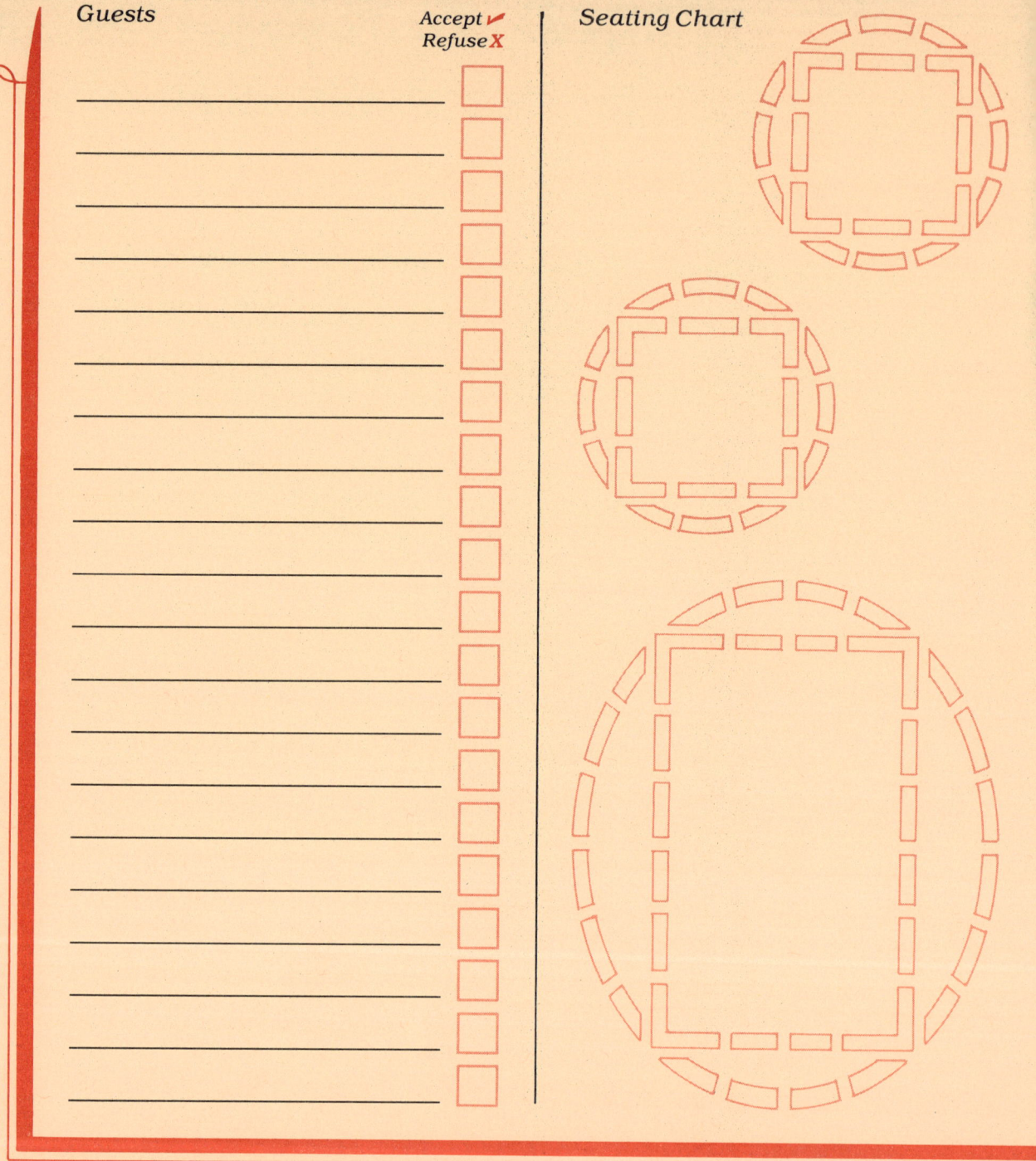

Occasion _____

Place _____

Day _____

Date _____ Time _____

Checklist:

- ☐ Invitations _____
- ☐ Reminders _____
- ☐ Menu _____
- ☐ Table Linens _____
- ☐ China _____
  _____
- ☐ Crystal _____
- ☐ Silver _____
  _____
- ☐ Serving Pieces _____
  _____
- ☐ Flowers _____
- ☐ Table Decorations _____
  _____
- ☐ Candles _____
- ☐ Place Cards _____
- ☐ Favors _____
  _____
- ☐ Shopping List _____

Rentals _____
_____

Help _____
_____

Costs:	Budgeted	Actual
Food	_____	_____
Wine	_____	_____
Liquor	_____	_____
Flowers	_____	_____
Rentals	_____	_____
Help	_____	_____
Other	_____	_____

Menu

Wines:

_____

Liquor and Liqueurs:

_____

Dress:
  Hostess _____
  Host _____

Review:

_____

Guests

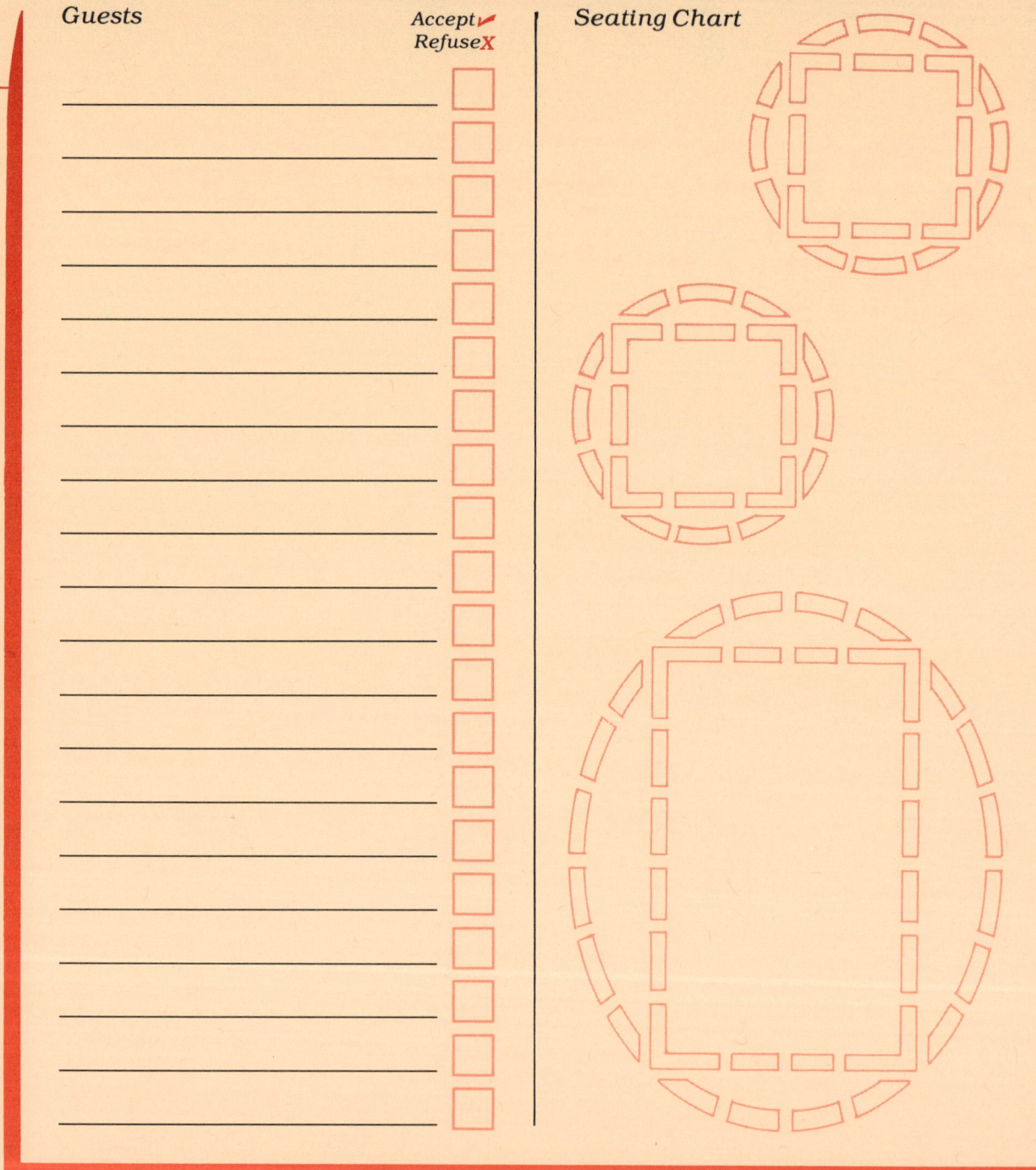

Accept ✔
Refuse **X**

Seating Chart

Occasion _____

Place _____

Day _____

Date _____ *Time* _____

Checklist:

☐ *Invitations* _____

☐ *Reminders* _____

☐ *Menu* _____

☐ *Table Linens* _____

☐ *China* _____

    _____

☐ *Crystal* _____

☐ *Silver* _____

    _____

☐ *Serving Pieces* _____

    _____

☐ *Flowers* _____

☐ *Table Decorations* _____

    _____

☐ *Candles* _____

☐ *Place Cards* _____

☐ *Favors* _____

    _____

☐ *Shopping List* _____

Rentals _____

_____

Help _____

_____

Costs:	*Budgeted*	*Actual*
Food	_____	_____
Wine	_____	_____
Liquor	_____	_____
Flowers	_____	_____
Rentals	_____	_____
Help	_____	_____
Other	_____	_____

Menu

Wines:

_____

Liquor and Liqueurs:

_____

Dress:

    Hostess _____

    Host _____

_____

Review:

_____

Guests

Accept ✔
Refuse **X**

Seating Chart

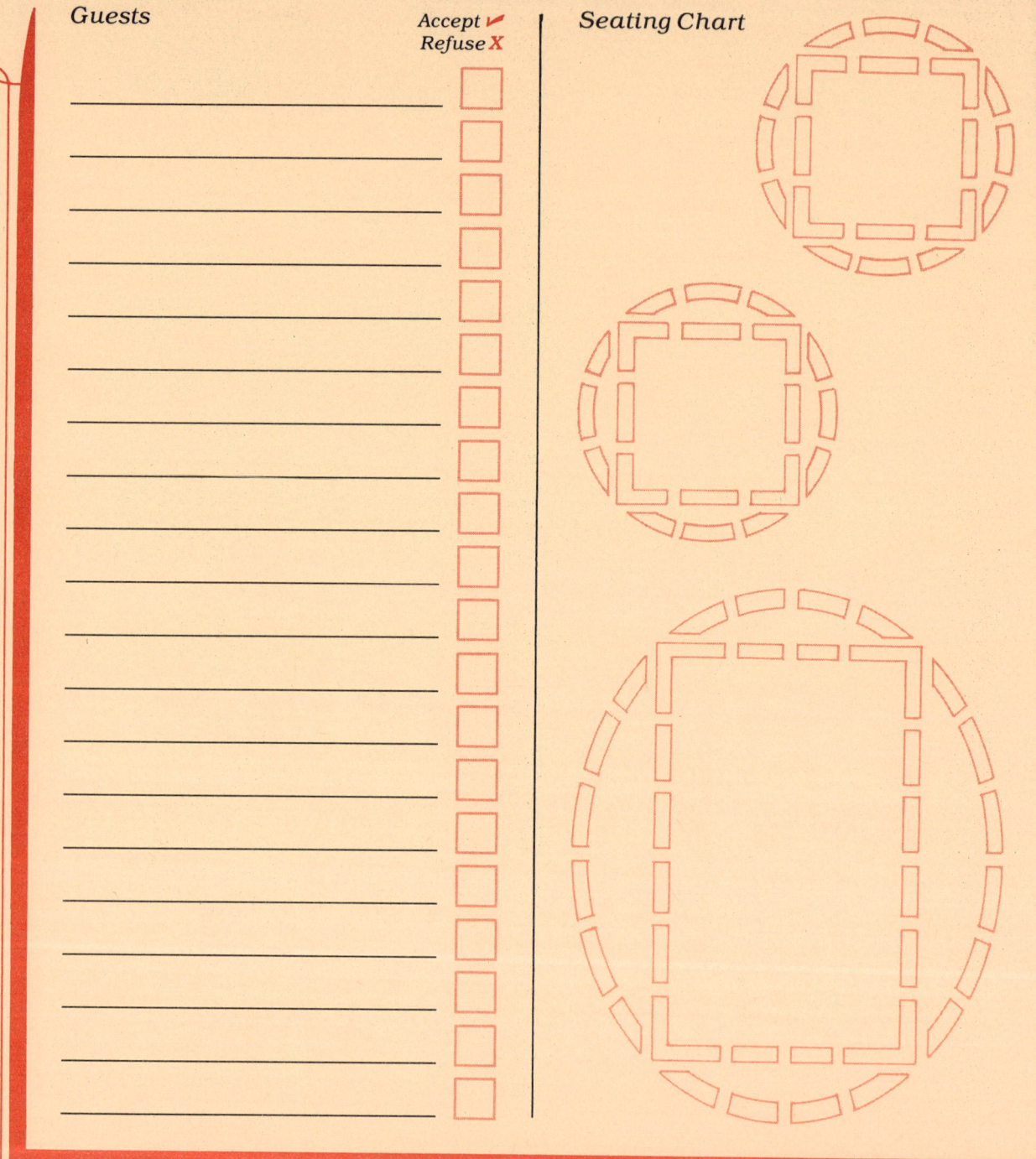

Occasion _____

Place _____

Day _____

Date _____ *Time* _____

Checklist:

☐ *Invitations* _____
☐ *Reminders* _____
☐ *Menu* _____
☐ *Table Linens* _____
☐ *China* _____
_____

☐ *Crystal* _____
☐ *Silver* _____
_____

☐ *Serving Pieces* _____
_____

☐ *Flowers* _____
☐ *Table Decorations* _____
_____

☐ *Candles* _____
☐ *Place Cards* _____
☐ *Favors* _____
_____

☐ *Shopping List* _____

Rentals _____
_____

Help _____
_____

Costs:	*Budgeted*	*Actual*
Food	_____	_____
Wine	_____	_____
Liquor	_____	_____
Flowers	_____	_____
Rentals	_____	_____
Help	_____	_____
Other	_____	_____

Menu

Wines:
_____

Liquor and Liqueurs:
_____

Dress:
  Hostess _____
  Host _____

Review:

_____

Guests

Accept ✔
Refuse **X**

Seating Chart

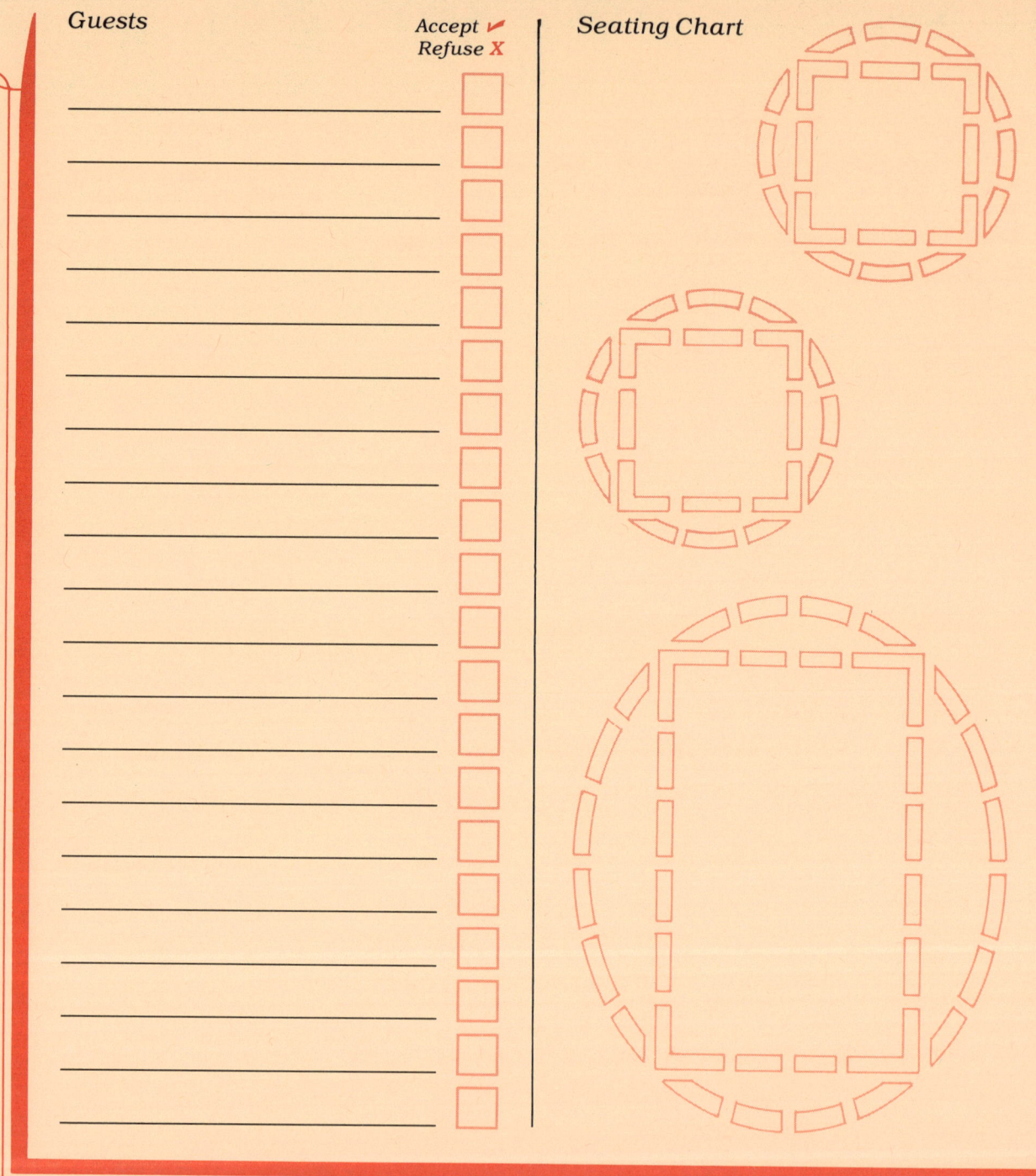

Occasion _____

Place _____

Day _____

Date _____ Time _____

Checklist:

- ☐ Invitations _____
- ☐ Reminders _____
- ☐ Menu _____
- ☐ Table Linens _____
- ☐ China _____

  _____

- ☐ Crystal _____
- ☐ Silver _____

  _____

- ☐ Serving Pieces _____

  _____

- ☐ Flowers _____
- ☐ Table Decorations _____

  _____

- ☐ Candles _____
- ☐ Place Cards _____
- ☐ Favors _____

  _____

- ☐ Shopping List _____

Rentals _____

_____

Help _____

_____

Costs:	Budgeted	Actual
Food	_____	_____
Wine	_____	_____
Liquor	_____	_____
Flowers	_____	_____
Rentals	_____	_____
Help	_____	_____
Other	_____	_____

Menu

Wines:

_____

Liquor and Liqueurs:

_____

Dress:
Hostess _____
Host _____

_____

Review:

_____

Guests

Accept ✔
Refuse ✗

Seating Chart

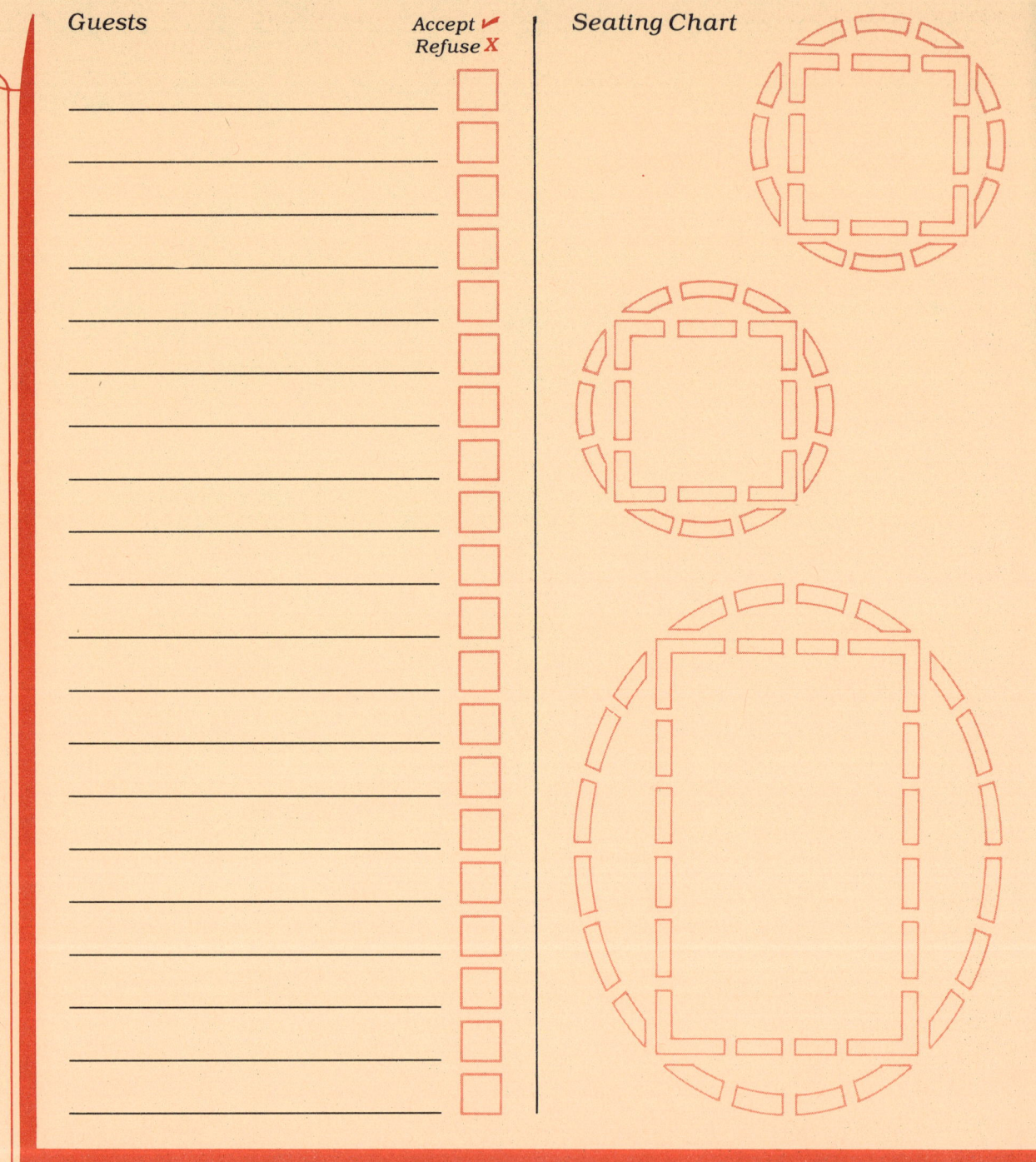

Occasion _____

Place _____

Day _____

Date _____Time _____

Checklist:

☐ Invitations_____
☐ Reminders _____
☐ Menu _____
☐ Table Linens_____
☐ China_____
   _____

☐ Crystal _____
☐ Silver _____
   _____

☐ Serving Pieces_____
   _____

☐ Flowers _____
☐ Table Decorations_____
   _____

☐ Candles_____
☐ Place Cards _____
☐ Favors_____
   _____

☐ Shopping List_____

Rentals _____
   _____

Help _____
   _____

Costs:	Budgeted	Actual
Food	_____	_____
Wine	_____	_____
Liquor	_____	_____
Flowers	_____	_____
Rentals	_____	_____
Help	_____	_____
Other	_____	_____

Menu

Wines:

Liquor and Liqueurs:

Dress:
   Hostess _____
   Host _____

Review:

Guests

Seating Chart

Occasion _____

Place _____

Day _____

Date _____ Time _____

Checklist:

☐ Invitations _____

☐ Reminders _____

☐ Menu _____

☐ Table Linens _____

☐ China _____

_____

☐ Crystal _____

☐ Silver _____

_____

☐ Serving Pieces _____

_____

☐ Flowers _____

☐ Table Decorations _____

_____

☐ Candles _____

☐ Place Cards _____

☐ Favors _____

_____

☐ Shopping List _____

Rentals _____

_____

Help _____

_____

Costs:	Budgeted	Actual
Food	_____	_____
Wine	_____	_____
Liquor	_____	_____
Flowers	_____	_____
Rentals	_____	_____
Help	_____	_____
Other	_____	_____

Menu

Wines: _____

_____

Liquor and Liqueurs: _____

_____

Dress:
  Hostess _____
  Host _____

_____

Review:

_____

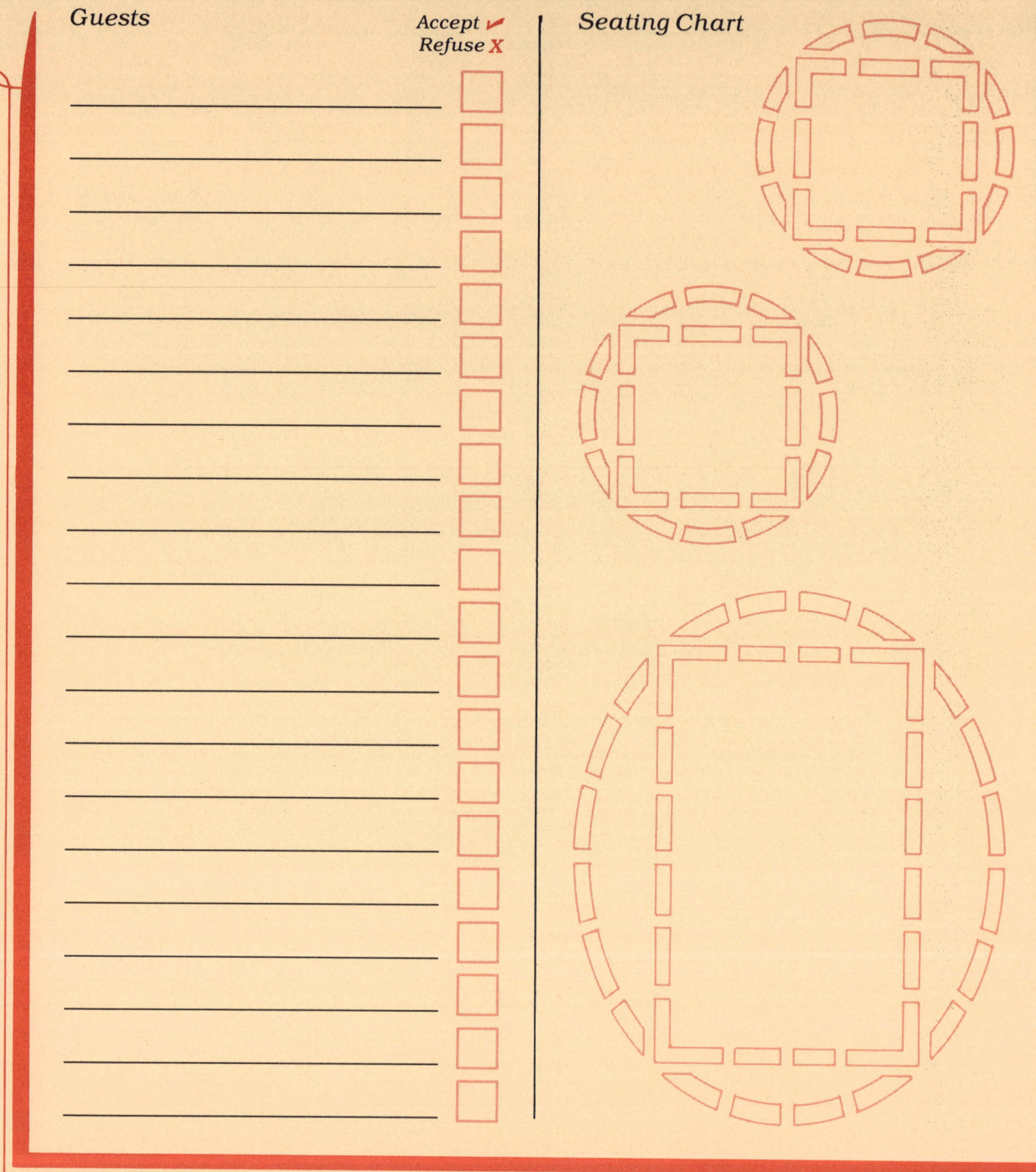

Guests

Accept ✔
Refuse ✗

Seating Chart

Occasion _____

Place _____

Day _____

Date _____ Time _____

Checklist:

- ☐ Invitations _____
- ☐ Reminders _____
- ☐ Menu _____
- ☐ Table Linens _____
- ☐ China _____

  _____
- ☐ Crystal _____
- ☐ Silver _____

  _____
- ☐ Serving Pieces _____

  _____
- ☐ Flowers _____
- ☐ Table Decorations _____

  _____
- ☐ Candles _____
- ☐ Place Cards _____
- ☐ Favors _____

  _____
- ☐ Shopping List _____

Rentals _____

_____

Help _____

_____

Costs:	Budgeted	Actual
Food	_____	_____
Wine	_____	_____
Liquor	_____	_____
Flowers	_____	_____
Rentals	_____	_____
Help	_____	_____
Other	_____	_____

Menu

Wines:

_____

Liquor and Liqueurs:

_____

Dress:
  Hostess _____
  Host _____

Review:

_____

Guests

Accept ✔
Refuse **X**

Seating Chart

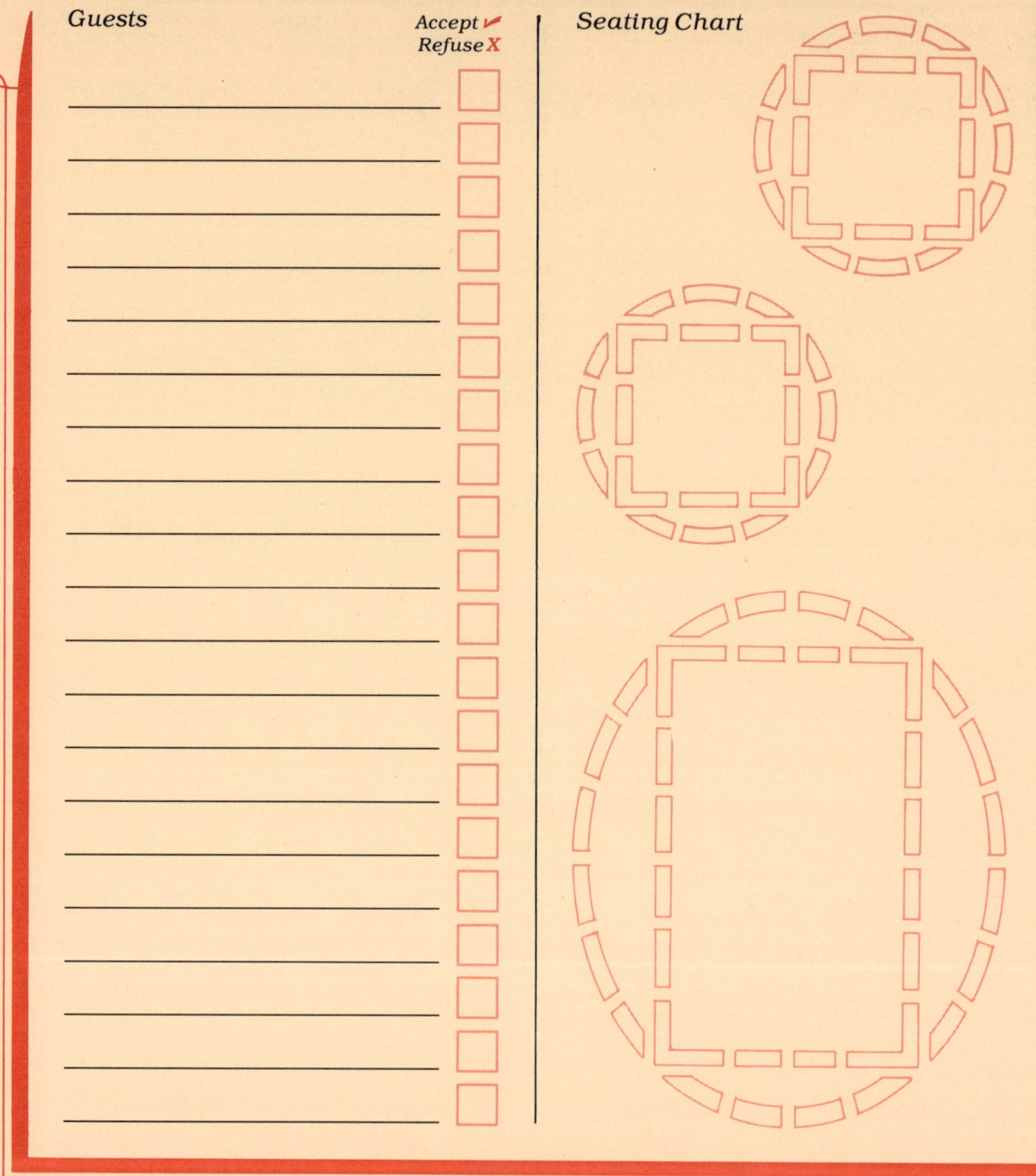

Occasion _____

Place _____

Day _____

Date _____ Time _____

Checklist:

☐ Invitations _____
☐ Reminders _____
☐ Menu _____
☐ Table Linens _____
☐ China _____
_____
☐ Crystal _____
☐ Silver _____
_____
☐ Serving Pieces _____
_____
☐ Flowers _____
☐ Table Decorations _____
_____
☐ Candles _____
☐ Place Cards _____
☐ Favors _____
_____
☐ Shopping List _____

Rentals _____
_____

Help _____
_____

Costs:	Budgeted	Actual
Food	_____	_____
Wine	_____	_____
Liquor	_____	_____
Flowers	_____	_____
Rentals	_____	_____
Help	_____	_____
Other	_____	_____

Menu

Wines:

_____
Liquor and Liqueurs:

_____
Dress:
Hostess _____
Host _____

_____
Review:

_____

Guests

Accept ✔
Refuse **X**

Seating Chart

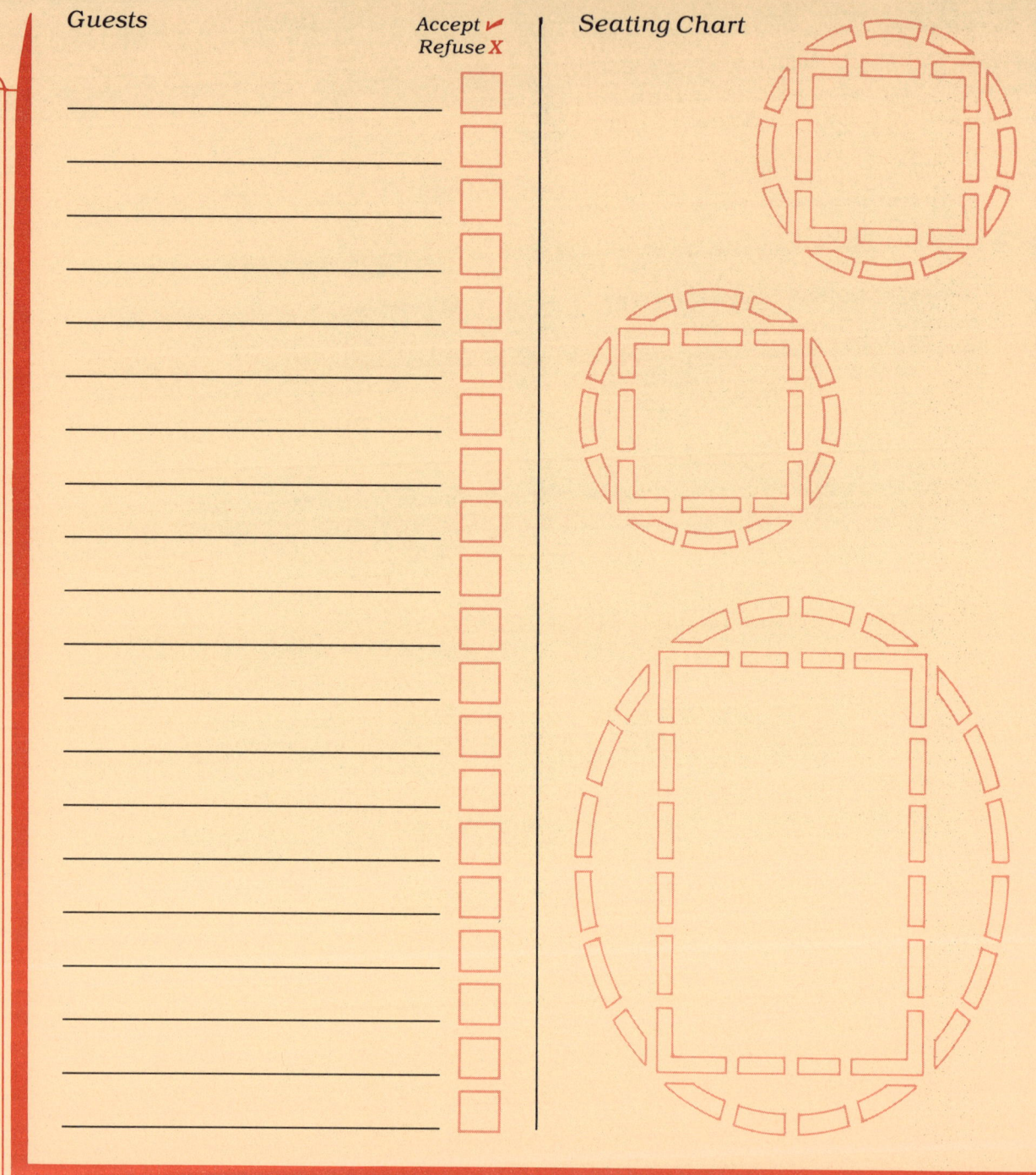

Occasion _____

Place _____

Day _____

Date _____Time _____

Checklist:

☐ Invitations_____

☐ Reminders _____

☐ Menu _____

☐ Table Linens_____

☐ China_____
_____

☐ Crystal _____

☐ Silver _____
_____

☐ Serving Pieces_____
_____

☐ Flowers _____

☐ Table Decorations_____
_____

☐ Candles_____

☐ Place Cards_____

☐ Favors_____
_____

☐ Shopping List_____

Rentals _____
_____

Help _____
_____

Costs:	Budgeted	Actual
Food	_____	_____
Wine	_____	_____
Liquor	_____	_____
Flowers	_____	_____
Rentals	_____	_____
Help	_____	_____
Other	_____	_____

Menu

Wines:

Liquor and Liqueurs:

Dress:
  Hostess _____
  Host _____

Review:

Guests

Accept ✔
Refuse ✗

Seating Chart

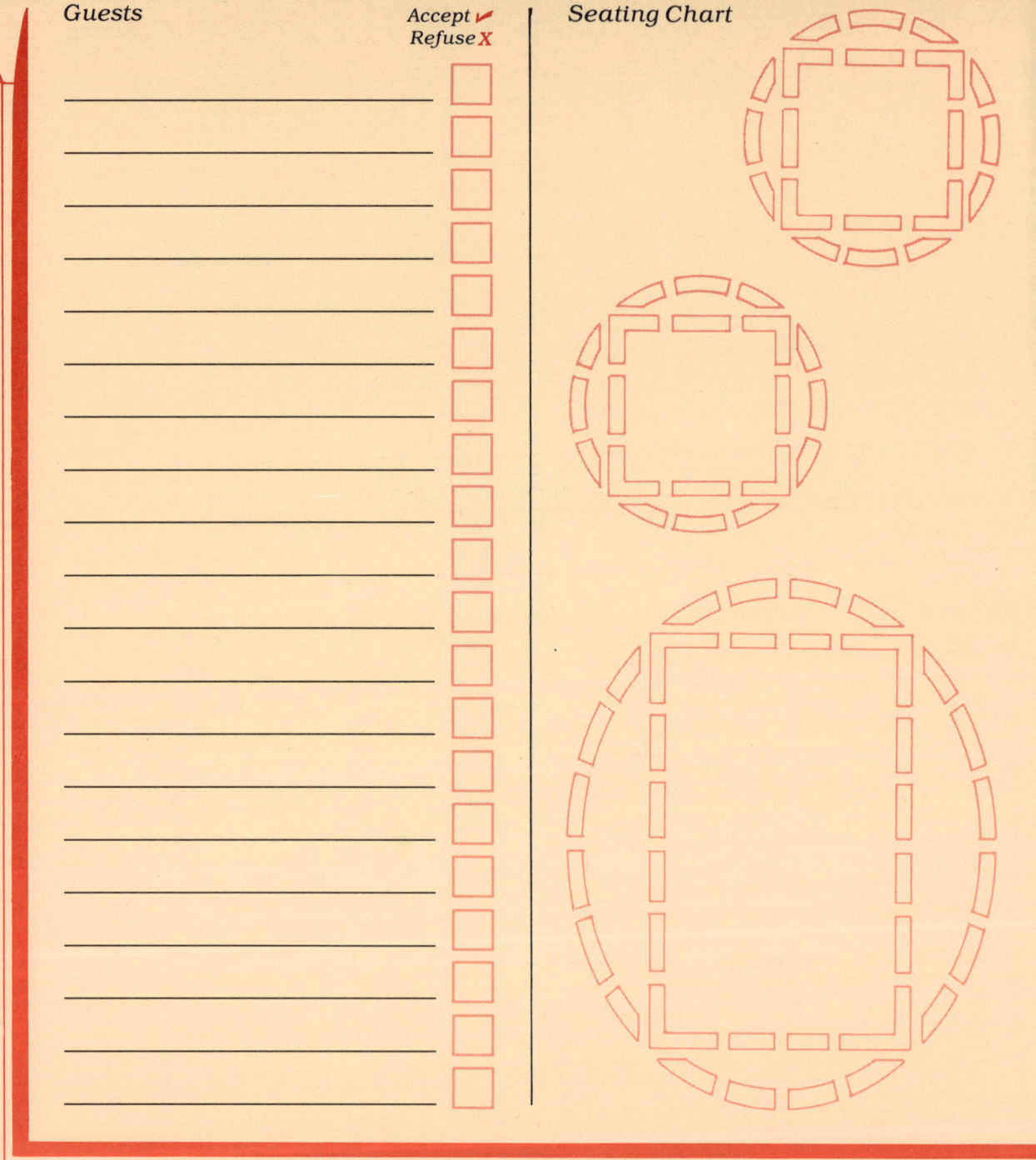

Occasion _____

Place _____

Day _____

Date _____ Time _____

Checklist:

- ☐ Invitations _____
- ☐ Reminders _____
- ☐ Menu _____
- ☐ Table Linens _____
- ☐ China _____

  _____

- ☐ Crystal _____
- ☐ Silver _____

  _____

- ☐ Serving Pieces _____

  _____

- ☐ Flowers _____
- ☐ Table Decorations _____

  _____

- ☐ Candles _____
- ☐ Place Cards _____
- ☐ Favors _____

  _____

- ☐ Shopping List _____

Rentals _____

_____

Help _____

_____

Costs:	Budgeted	Actual
Food	_____	_____
Wine	_____	_____
Liquor	_____	_____
Flowers	_____	_____
Rentals	_____	_____
Help	_____	_____
Other	_____	_____

Menu

Wines:

_____

Liquor and Liqueurs:

_____

Dress:

  Hostess _____

  Host _____

_____

Review:

_____

Guests

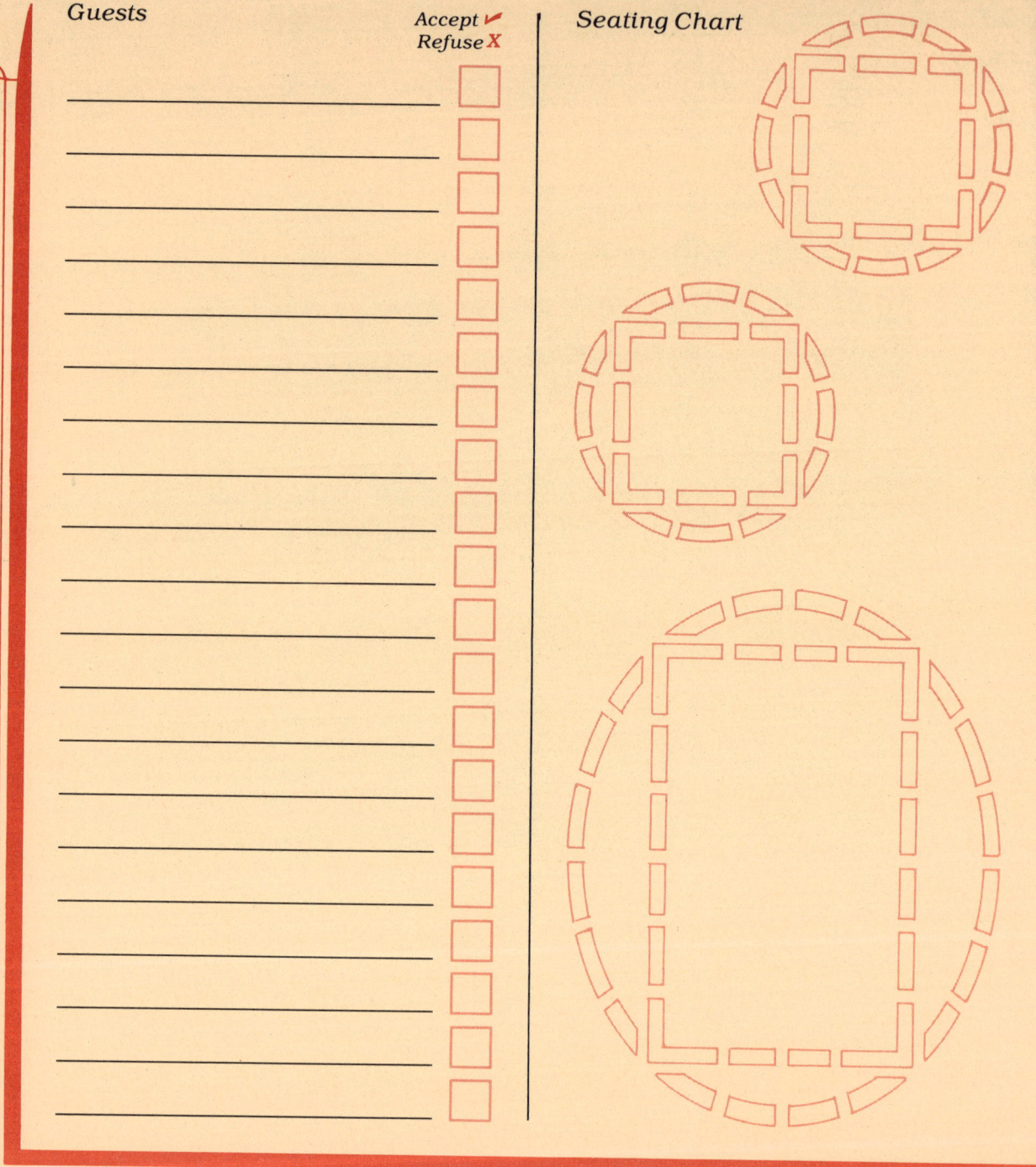

Accept ✔
Refuse ✗

Seating Chart

Occasion _____

Place _____

Day _____

Date _____ *Time* _____

Checklist:

☐ *Invitations* _____

☐ *Reminders* _____

☐ *Menu* _____

☐ *Table Linens* _____

☐ *China* _____

_____

☐ *Crystal* _____

☐ *Silver* _____

_____

☐ *Serving Pieces* _____

_____

☐ *Flowers* _____

☐ *Table Decorations* _____

_____

☐ *Candles* _____

☐ *Place Cards* _____

☐ *Favors* _____

_____

☐ *Shopping List* _____

Rentals _____

_____

Help _____

_____

Costs:	*Budgeted*	*Actual*
Food	_____	_____
Wine	_____	_____
Liquor	_____	_____
Flowers	_____	_____
Rentals	_____	_____
Help	_____	_____
Other	_____	_____

Menu

Wines:

_____

Liquor and Liqueurs:

_____

Dress:
   Hostess _____
   Host _____

Review:

_____

Guests

Accept ✔
Refuse X

Seating Chart

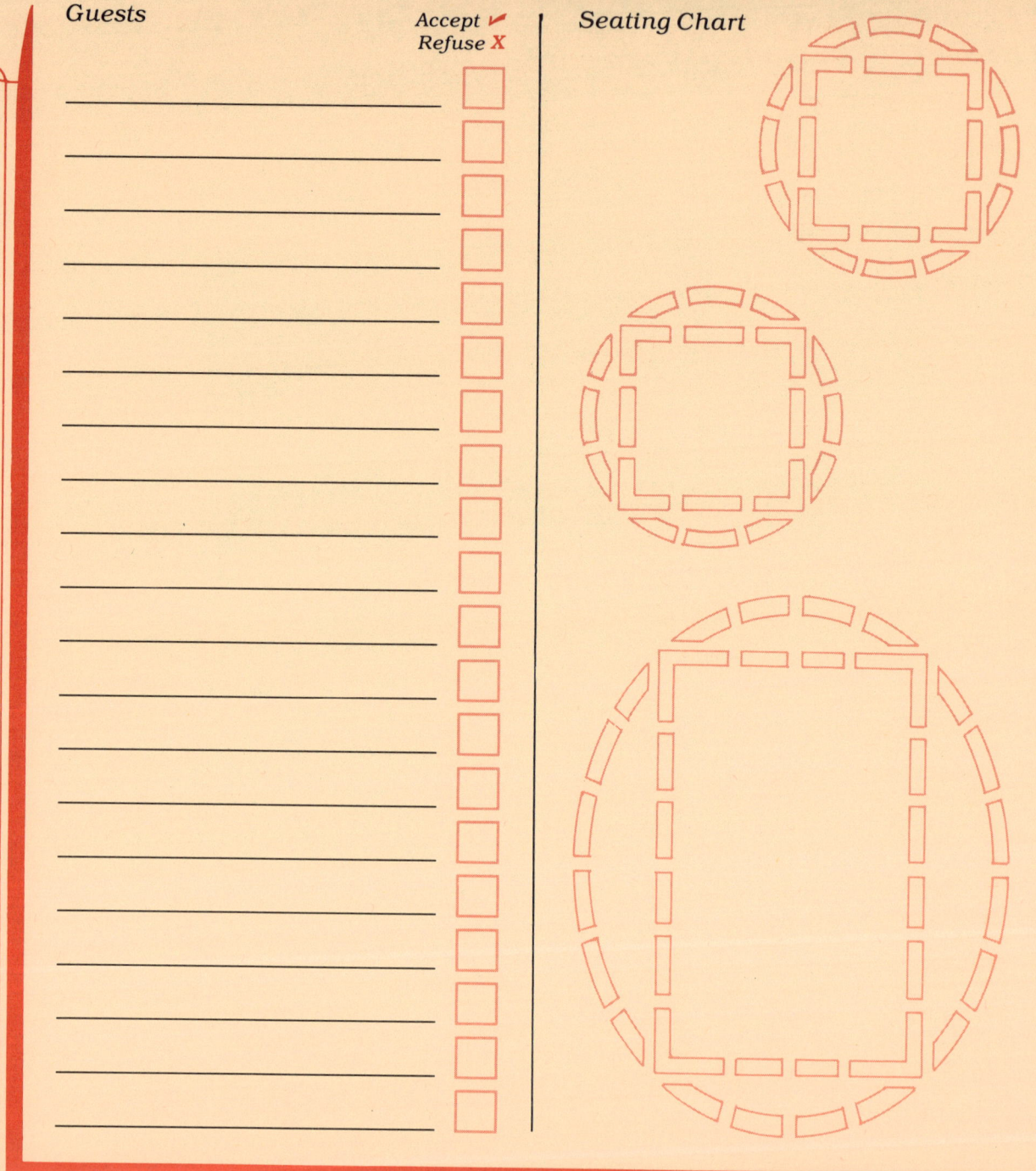

Occasion _____

Place _____

Day _____

Date _____ *Time* _____

Checklist:

☐ *Invitations* _____

☐ *Reminders* _____

☐ *Menu* _____

☐ *Table Linens* _____

☐ *China* _____

_____

☐ *Crystal* _____

☐ *Silver* _____

_____

☐ *Serving Pieces* _____

_____

☐ *Flowers* _____

☐ *Table Decorations* _____

_____

☐ *Candles* _____

☐ *Place Cards* _____

☐ *Favors* _____

☐ *Shopping List* _____

Rentals _____

_____

Help _____

Costs:	*Budgeted*	*Actual*
Food	_____	_____
Wine	_____	_____
Liquor	_____	_____
Flowers	_____	_____
Rentals	_____	_____
Help	_____	_____
Other	_____	_____

Menu

Wines:

_____

Liquor and Liqueurs:

_____

Dress:

Hostess _____

Host _____

Review:

_____

Guests

Seating Chart

Accept ✔
Refuse X

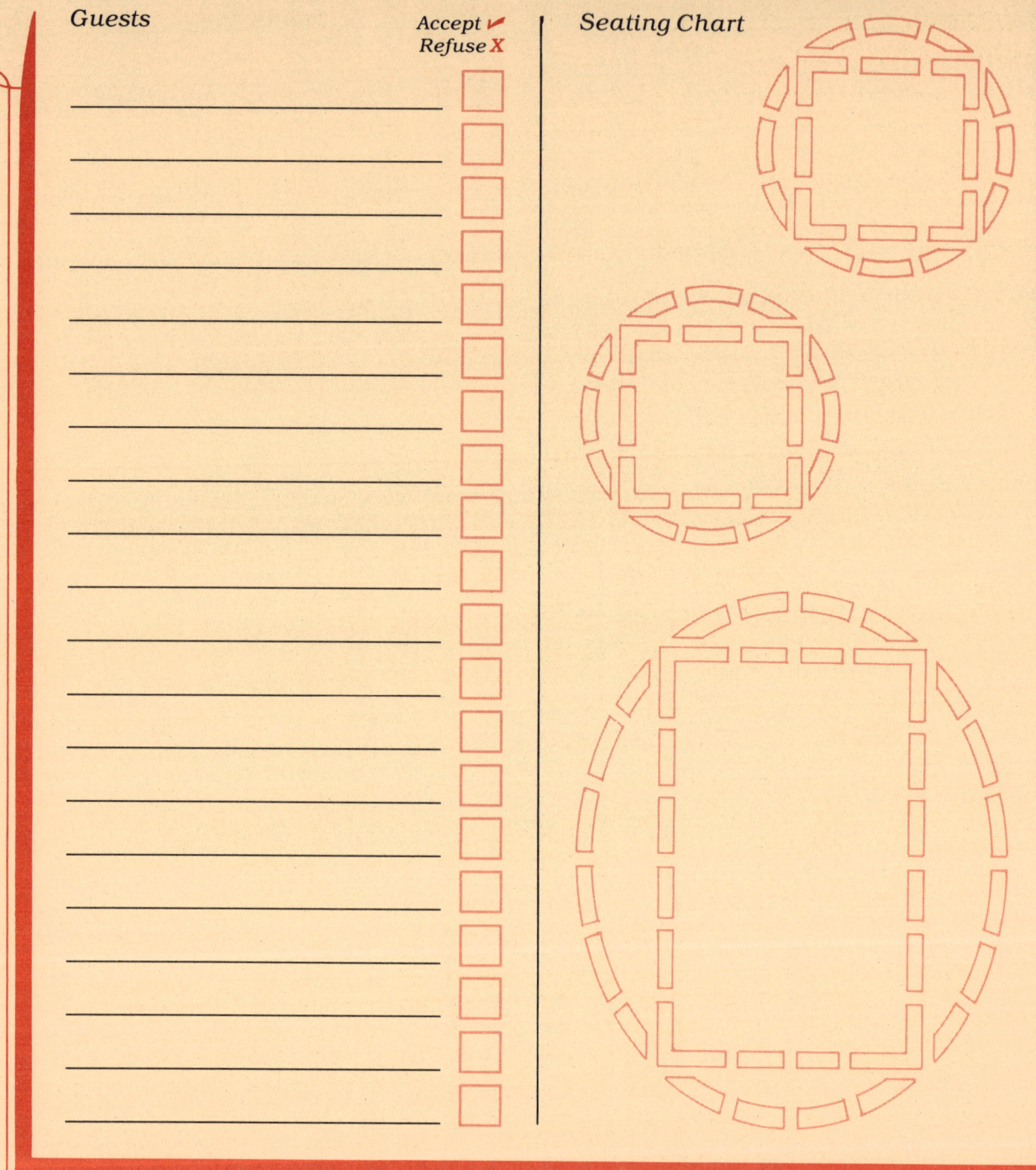

Occasion _____

Place _____

Day _____

Date _____ Time _____

Checklist:

☐ Invitations _____
☐ Reminders _____
☐ Menu _____
☐ Table Linens _____
☐ China _____
_____
☐ Crystal _____
☐ Silver _____
_____
☐ Serving Pieces _____
_____
☐ Flowers _____
☐ Table Decorations _____
_____
☐ Candles _____
☐ Place Cards _____
☐ Favors _____
_____
☐ Shopping List _____

Rentals _____
_____

Help _____
_____

Costs:	Budgeted	Actual
Food	_____	_____
Wine	_____	_____
Liquor	_____	_____
Flowers	_____	_____
Rentals	_____	_____
Help	_____	_____
Other	_____	_____

Menu

Wines:

_____

Liquor and Liqueurs:

_____

Dress:
  Hostess _____
  Host _____

Review:

_____

Guests

Seating Chart

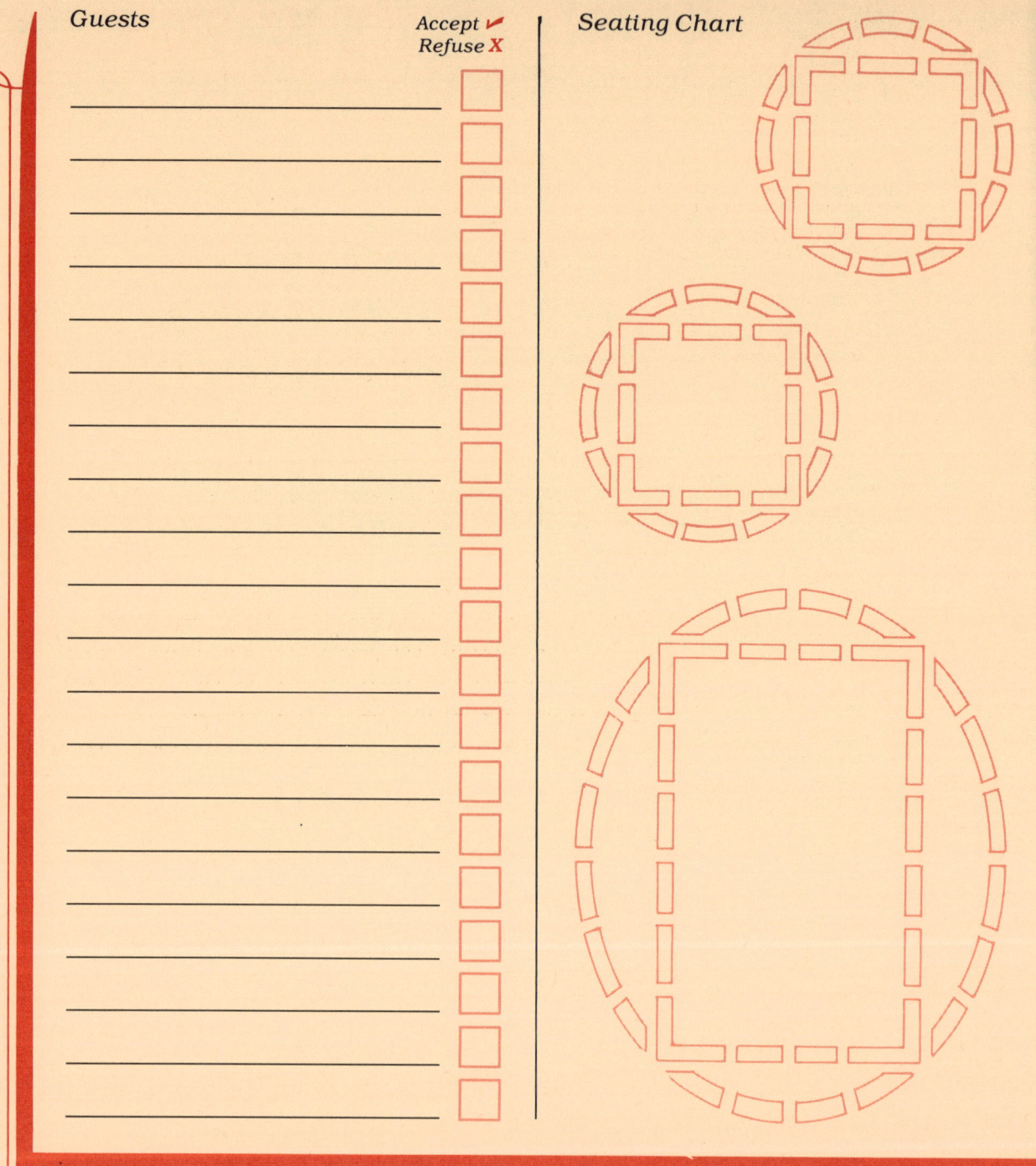

Occasion _____

Place _____

Day _____

Date _____ Time _____

Checklist:

- ☐ Invitations _____
- ☐ Reminders _____
- ☐ Menu _____
- ☐ Table Linens _____
- ☐ China _____
      _____
- ☐ Crystal _____
- ☐ Silver _____
      _____
- ☐ Serving Pieces _____
      _____
- ☐ Flowers _____
- ☐ Table Decorations _____
      _____
- ☐ Candles _____
- ☐ Place Cards _____
- ☐ Favors _____
      _____
- ☐ Shopping List _____

Rentals _____
      _____

Help _____

Costs:	Budgeted	Actual
Food	_____	_____
Wine	_____	_____
Liquor	_____	_____
Flowers	_____	_____
Rentals	_____	_____
Help	_____	_____
Other	_____	_____

Menu

Wines:

Liquor and Liqueurs:

Dress:
  Hostess _____
  Host _____

Review:

Guests

Accept ✔
Refuse ✗

_____

_____

_____

_____

_____

_____

_____

_____

_____

_____

_____

_____

_____

_____

_____

_____

_____

_____

Seating Chart

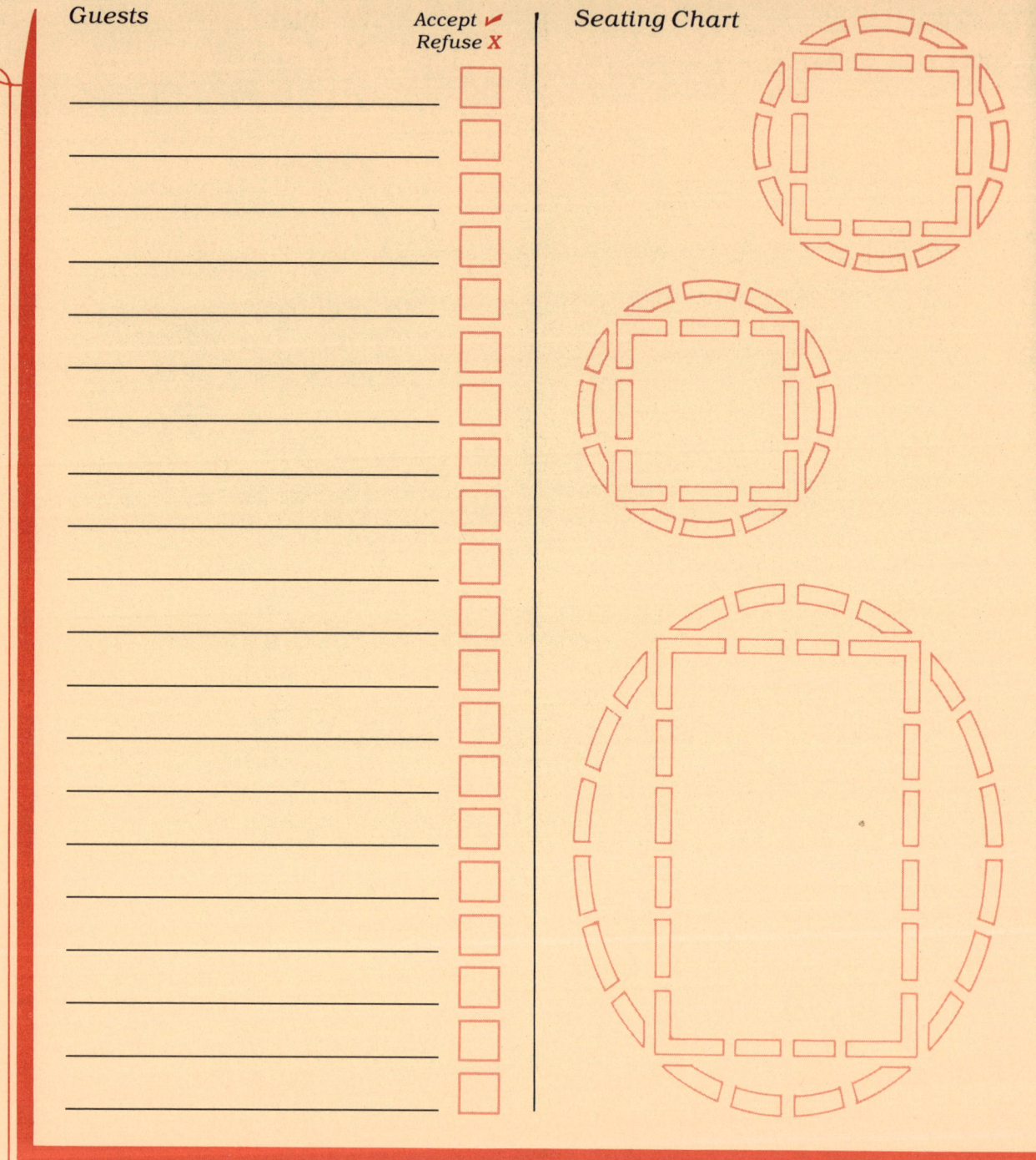

Occasion _____

Place _____

Day _____

Date _____Time _____

Checklist:

☐ *Invitations*_____

☐ *Reminders* _____

☐ *Menu* _____

☐ *Table Linens*_____

☐ *China*_____

   _____

☐ *Crystal* _____

☐ *Silver* _____

   _____

☐ *Serving Pieces*_____

   _____

☐ *Flowers* _____

☐ *Table Decorations*_____

   _____

☐ *Candles*_____

☐ *Place Cards* _____

☐ *Favors*_____

   _____

☐ *Shopping List*_____

Rentals _____

_____

Help _____

_____

Costs:	*Budgeted*	*Actual*
Food	_____	_____
Wine	_____	_____
Liquor	_____	_____
Flowers	_____	_____
Rentals	_____	_____
Help	_____	_____
Other	_____	_____

Menu

Wines:

_____

Liquor and Liqueurs:

_____

Dress:

   Hostess _____

   Host _____

Review:

_____

Guests

_____

_____

_____

_____

_____

_____

_____

_____

_____

_____

_____

_____

_____

_____

_____

_____

_____

_____

Accept ✔
Refuse X

Seating Chart

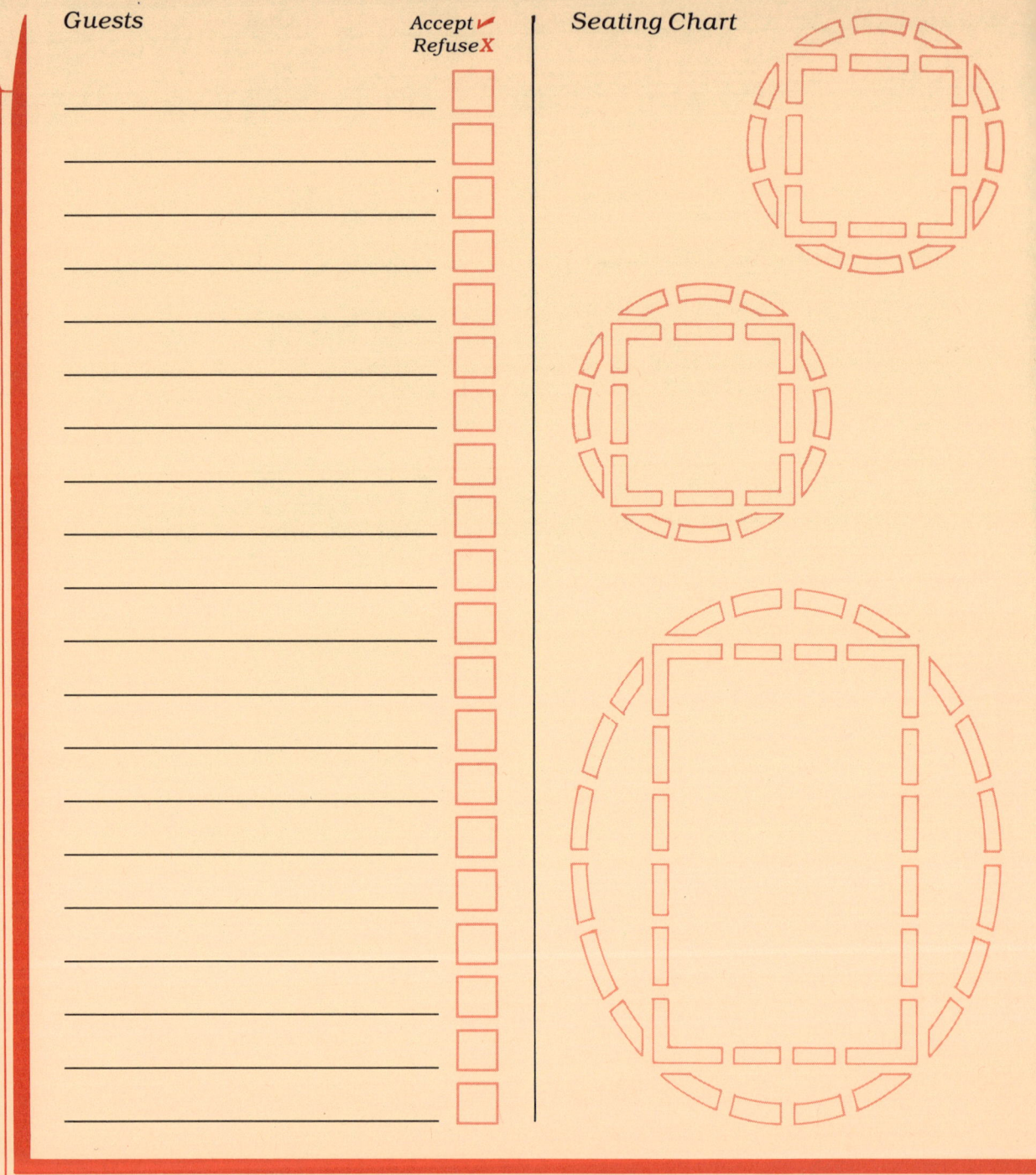

Occasion _____

Place _____

Day _____

Date _____ Time _____

Checklist:

- ☐ Invitations _____
- ☐ Reminders _____
- ☐ Menu _____
- ☐ Table Linens _____
- ☐ China _____
  _____
- ☐ Crystal _____
- ☐ Silver _____
  _____
- ☐ Serving Pieces _____
  _____
- ☐ Flowers _____
- ☐ Table Decorations _____
  _____
- ☐ Candles _____
- ☐ Place Cards _____
- ☐ Favors _____
  _____
- ☐ Shopping List _____

Rentals _____
_____

Help _____

Costs:	Budgeted	Actual
Food	_____	_____
Wine	_____	_____
Liquor	_____	_____
Flowers	_____	_____
Rentals	_____	_____
Help	_____	_____
Other	_____	_____

Menu

Wines:

_____

Liquor and Liqueurs:

_____

Dress:
   Hostess _____
   Host _____

Review:

_____

Guests

Accept ✔
Refuse X

_____	☐
_____	☐
_____	☐
_____	☐
_____	☐
_____	☐
_____	☐
_____	☐
_____	☐
_____	☐
_____	☐
_____	☐
_____	☐
_____	☐
_____	☐
_____	☐
_____	☐
_____	☐
_____	☐

Seating Chart

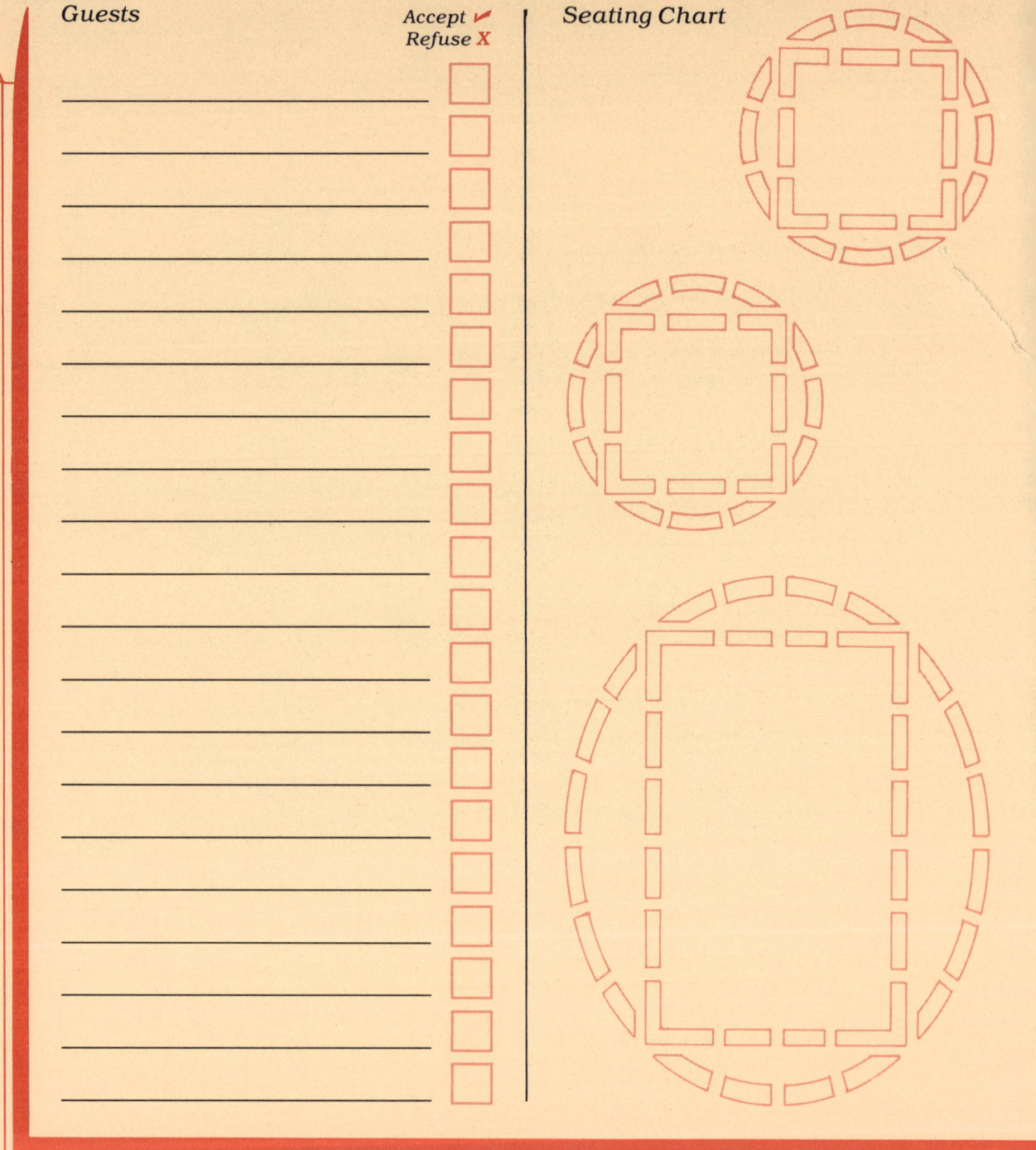

Occasion _____

Place _____

Day _____

Date _____ Time _____

Checklist:

☐ Invitations _____

☐ Reminders _____

☐ Menu _____

☐ Table Linens _____

☐ China _____

_____

☐ Crystal _____

☐ Silver _____

_____

☐ Serving Pieces _____

_____

☐ Flowers _____

☐ Table Decorations _____

_____

☐ Candles _____

☐ Place Cards _____

☐ Favors _____

_____

☐ Shopping List _____

Rentals _____

_____

Help _____

_____

Costs:	Budgeted	Actual
Food	_____	_____
Wine	_____	_____
Liquor	_____	_____
Flowers	_____	_____
Rentals	_____	_____
Help	_____	_____
Other	_____	_____

Menu

Wines:

_____

Liquor and Liqueurs:

_____

Dress:
  Hostess _____
  Host _____

_____

Review:

_____

Guests

_____

_____

_____

_____

_____

_____

_____

_____

_____

_____

_____

_____

_____

_____

_____

_____

_____

_____

_____

Accept ✔
Refuse X

Seating Chart

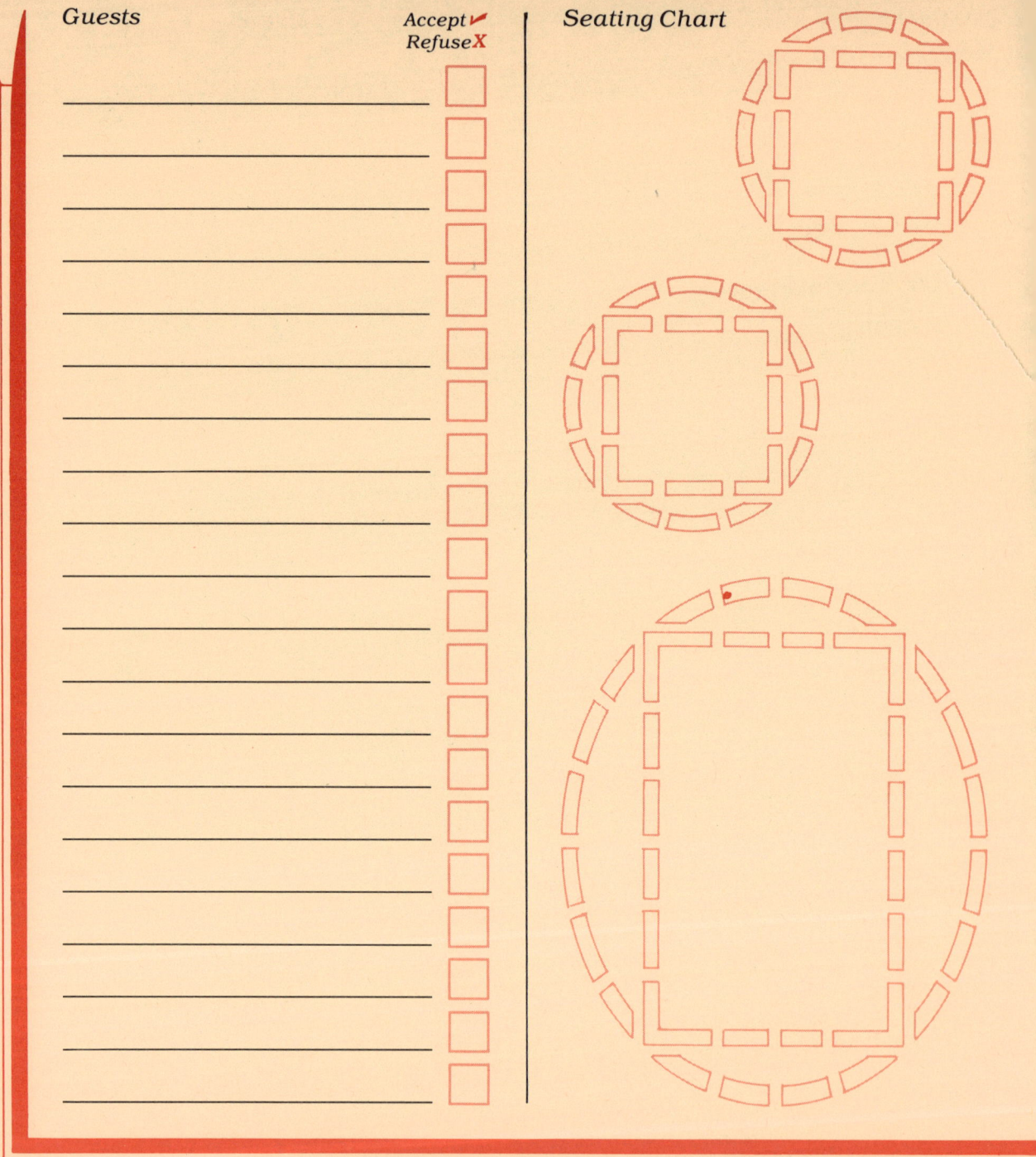

Occasion _____

Place _____

Day _____

Date _____ Time _____

Checklist:

☐ Invitations _____
☐ Reminders _____
☐ Menu _____
☐ Table Linens _____
☐ China _____

_____

☐ Crystal _____
☐ Silver _____

_____

☐ Serving Pieces _____

_____

☐ Flowers _____
☐ Table Decorations _____

_____

☐ Candles _____
☐ Place Cards _____
☐ Favors _____

☐ Shopping List _____

Rentals _____

_____

Help _____

Costs:	Budgeted	Actual
Food	_____	_____
Wine	_____	_____
Liquor	_____	_____
Flowers	_____	_____
Rentals	_____	_____
Help	_____	_____
Other	_____	_____

Menu

Wines:

_____

Liquor and Liqueurs:

_____

Dress:
   Hostess _____
   Host _____

_____

Review:

_____

Guests

Accept ✔
Refuse **X**

Seating Chart

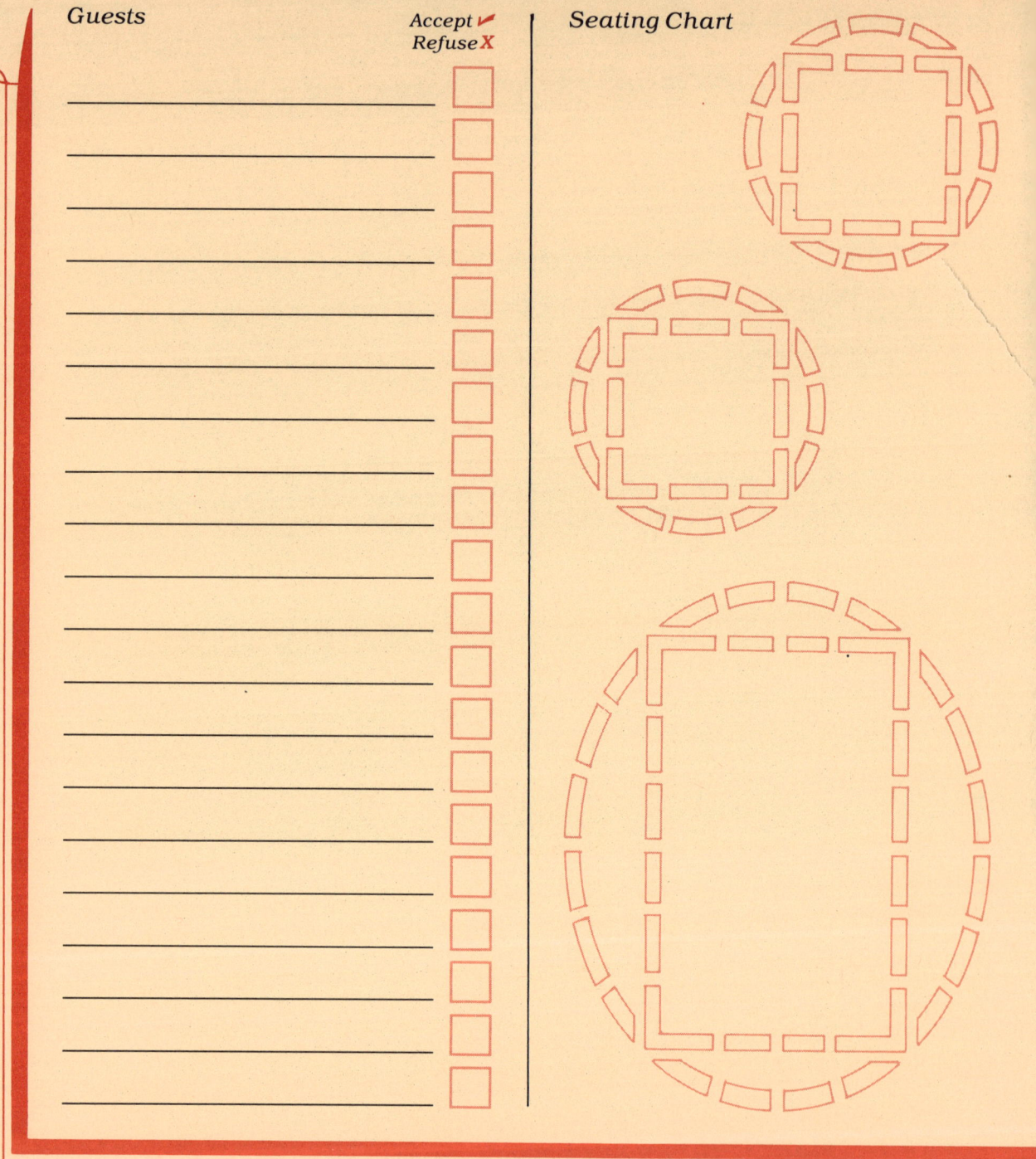

Occasion _____

Place _____

Day _____

Date _____ Time _____

Checklist:

☐ Invitations _____
☐ Reminders _____
☐ Menu _____
☐ Table Linens _____
☐ China _____
_____
☐ Crystal _____
☐ Silver _____
_____
☐ Serving Pieces _____
_____
☐ Flowers _____
☐ Table Decorations _____
_____
☐ Candles _____
☐ Place Cards _____
☐ Favors _____
_____
☐ Shopping List _____

Rentals _____
_____

Help _____
_____

Costs:	Budgeted	Actual
Food	_____	_____
Wine	_____	_____
Liquor	_____	_____
Flowers	_____	_____
Rentals	_____	_____
Help	_____	_____
Other	_____	_____

Menu

Wines:

_____

Liquor and Liqueurs:

_____

Dress:
  Hostess _____
  Host _____

Review:

Guests

Accept ✔
Refuse ✗

Seating Chart

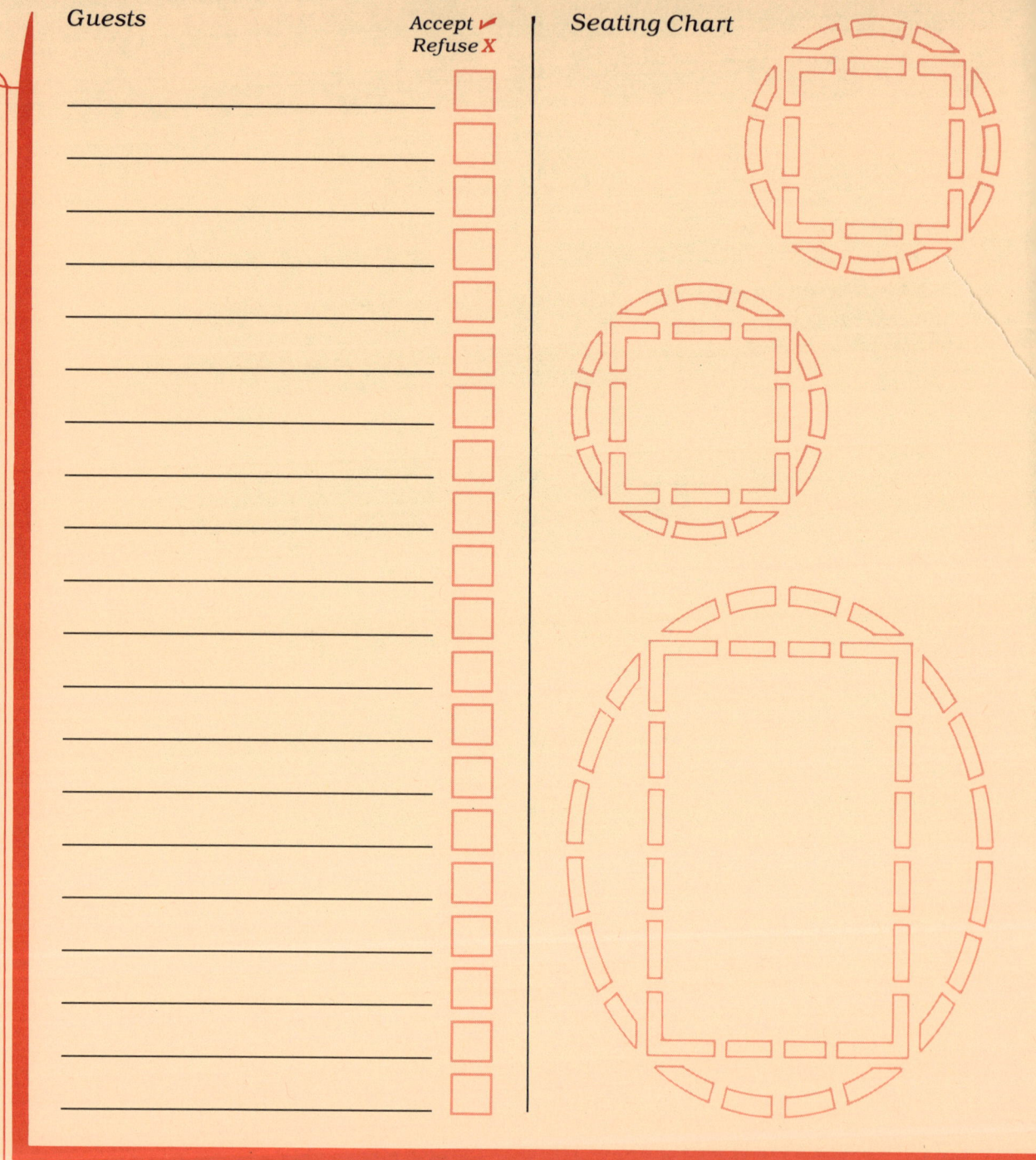

Occasion _____

Place _____

Day _____

Date _____ Time _____

Checklist:

☐ Invitations _____

☐ Reminders _____

☐ Menu _____

☑ Table Linens _____

☐ China _____

_____

☐ Crystal _____

☐ Silver _____

_____

☐ Serving Pieces _____

_____

☐ Flowers _____

☐ Table Decorations _____

_____

☐ Candles _____

☐ Place Cards _____

☐ Favors _____

_____

☐ Shopping List _____

Rentals _____

_____

Help _____

Costs:	Budgeted	Actual
Food	_____	_____
Wine	_____	_____
Liquor	_____	_____
Flowers	_____	_____
Rentals	_____	_____
Help	_____	_____
Other	_____	_____

Menu

Wines:

_____

Liquor and Liqueurs:

_____

Dress:
   Hostess _____
   Host _____

Review:

_____

Guests

Seating Chart

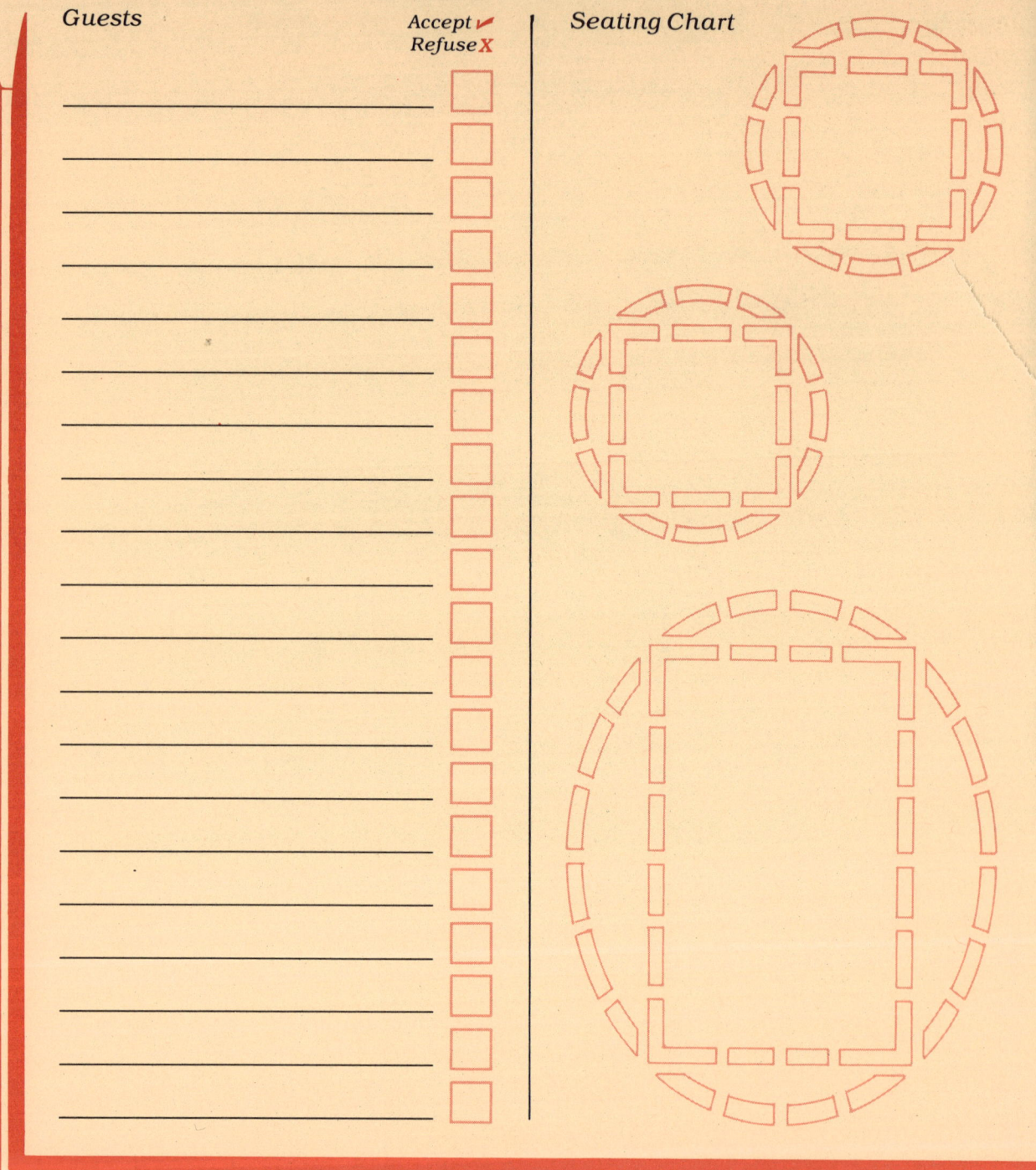

Occasion _____

Place _____

Day _____

Date _____ Time _____

Checklist:

☐ Invitations _____
☐ Reminders _____
☐ Menu _____
☐ Table Linens _____
☐ China _____
   _____
☐ Crystal _____
☐ Silver _____
   _____
☐ Serving Pieces _____
   _____
☐ Flowers _____
☐ Table Decorations _____
   _____
☐ Candles _____
☐ Place Cards _____
☐ Favors _____
   _____
☐ Shopping List _____

Rentals _____
_____

Help _____
_____

Costs:	Budgeted	Actual
Food	_____	_____
Wine	_____	_____
Liquor	_____	_____
Flowers	_____	_____
Rentals	_____	_____
Help	_____	_____
Other	_____	_____

Menu

Wines:

_____

Liquor and Liqueurs:

_____

Dress:
   Hostess _____
   Host _____

Review:

_____

Jeanne Jones has received international acclaim for her best-selling diet cookbooks. But actually it was her love of entertaining that motivated her to write these books for those who are concerned about diet. Jeanne's imaginative parties at her home in La Jolla, California, earned her the reputation of being one of the country's leading hostesses. She also serves as a party and menu consultant for several major food product manufacturers. Her other books are *The Calculating Cook: A Gourmet Cookbook for Diabetics and Dieters; Diet for a Happy Heart, A Low-Cholesterol Cookbook; The Fabulous Fiber Cookbook* and *Secrets of Salt-Free Cooking.*